Liturgy in the Shadows of Trauma

Liturgy in the Shadows of Trauma

Reckoning with the Roman Catholic Sex-Abuse Crisis

DAVID FARINA TURNBLOOM, MEGAN BREEN,
NOAH LAMBERGER, AND KATE TYSCHPER

Maryknoll, New York 10545

Founded in 1970, Orbis Books endeavors to publish works that enlighten the mind, nourish the spirit, and challenge the conscience. The publishing arm of the Maryknoll Fathers and Brothers, Orbis seeks to explore the global dimensions of the Christian faith and mission, to invite dialogue with diverse cultures and religious traditions, and to serve the cause of reconciliation and peace. The books published reflect the views of their authors and do not represent the official position of the Maryknoll Society. To learn more about Maryknoll and Orbis Books, please visit our website at www.orbisbooks.com.

Copyright © 2025 by David Farina Turnbloom, Megan Breen, Noah Lamberger, and Kate Tyschper.

Published by Orbis Books, Box 302, Maryknoll, NY 10545-0302.

All rights reserved.

All Vatican documents are available online at www.Vatican.va.

No part of this publication may be reproduced or transmitted in any form or by any means, electronic or mechanical, including photocopying, recording, or any information storage or retrieval system, without prior permission in writing from the publisher.

Queries regarding rights and permissions should be addressed to: Orbis Books, P.O. Box 302, Maryknoll, NY 10545-0302.

Manufactured in the United States of America.
Copyediting and typesetting by Joan Weber Laflamme.

Library of Congress Cataloging-in-Publication Data

Names: Turnbloom, David Farina author | Breen, Megan author | Lamberger, Noah author | Tyschper, Kate author
Title: Liturgy in the shadows of trauma : reckoning with the Roman Catholic sex abuse crisis / David Farina Turnbloom, Megan Breen, Noah Lamberger and Kate Tyschper.
Description: Maryknoll, NY : Orbis Books, [2025] | Includes bibliographical references and index.
Identifiers: LCCN 2025026952 (print) | LCCN 2025026953 (ebook) | ISBN 9781626986398 trade paperback | ISBN 9798888660942 epub
Subjects: LCSH: Catholic Church—Clergy—Sexual behavior | Catholic Church—Liturgy | Sexual abuse victims—Religious life
Classification: LCC BX1912.9 .T876 2025 (print) | LCC BX1912.9 (ebook)
LC record available at https://lccn.loc.gov/2025026952
LC ebook record available at https://lccn.loc.gov/2025026953

For my parents, Dan and Dorothy,
who were my very first sacraments.
—David

For my grandparents, Barb and Tom Tyschper,
for your unwavering support.
—Kate

For my father, Mark Lamberger,
and my grandmother, Juanita Lamberger.
For your spiritual example, guidance, and steadiness.
—Noah

For those whose lives were lost,
whose recollections fell upon unwilling ears.
For those who never had a chance to heal.
I honor your memory, and to you I dedicate each word.
May you never feel so alone.
—Megan

Contents

Acknowledgments   *xi*
Key Terms   *xiii*
Introduction   *xv*

1 Cultivating Grace through Liturgy   1
    What Is the Liturgy?   3
    Liturgy Dispensing Grace   12
    Liturgy Offering Grace   17
    Conclusion: Cultivating Grace through Liturgy   22

2 A Perversion of Power
Understanding Clericalist Culture   27
    Triumphalism: Clerics as Above and Apart   31
    Interchangeability: Clerics with Excessive
       Rights and Responsibilities   37
    Impunity: Clerics Demanding Excessive
       Trust and Authority   42
    Conclusion: Clericalism Facilitating Trauma   50

3 The Real Presence of Violence
PTSD and the Liturgy   53
    What Is Trauma?   54
    Post-Traumatic Stress Disorder   59
    PTSD Subverting Liturgical Efficacy   66
    Conclusion: Revealing a Culture of Death   73

4 Losing Faith
Moral Injury and the Liturgy 77
What Is Moral Injury? 78
Different Types of Moral Injury 85
Moral Injury Hindering Liturgical
    Efficacy 95
Conclusion: Losing Faith 101

5 Losing Hope
Moral Distress and the Liturgy 103
What Is Moral Distress? 106
Moral Distress and Clericalist Culture 110
Moral Distress Hindering Liturgical
    Efficacy 115
Conclusion: Church-Perpetuated Sexual
    Abuse 118

6 Toward a Relational Ordained Ministry 121
Ordained Ministry Rooted in Substance
    Ontology 123
Ordained Ministry Rooted in Relational
    Ontology 132
Preventing Abuse and Healing Trauma
    through Relational Ordained Ministry 137
Conclusion: The Gift of Authority 143

7 Avoiding Rhetorical Violence 147
Cycles of Abuse and Rhetorical
    Manipulation 148
Rhetorical Manipulation and the
    Liturgy 151
A Step Forward: Seeking Safety and
    Empowerment 159

8 Seeking Salvation outside the Church   169
    Mitigating Triumphalism: Finding Salvation
       outside the Church   172
    Subverting Triumphalism: No Salvation inside the
       Church   178
    Grieving a Loss   186
    Conclusion: Accepting Grace   192

Index   *195*

Acknowledgments

A great deal goes into writing any book. Our research team was founded on the belief that there is no such thing as an individual scholar. Every insight and every question that a person develops is the result of both seen and unseen grace. In light of that belief, we would like to acknowledge some people and institutions who have made this volume possible. To begin, we wish to thank all the past and current members of the Collaborative Humanities Investigating Religion and Power (CHIRP) Lab. Your work and dialogue have provided innumerable insights and helped us see scholarship as a fundamentally communal process. We also wish to thank the University of Portland's Summer Undergraduate Research Experience program for supporting our work and continuing to create space where faculty and students can be true collaborators. Additionally, we would like to thank the University of Portland's Garaventa Center, especially its former director, Karen Eifler, for continually providing a platform to refine and share our research. We would like to thank the members of the North American Academy of Liturgy who participate in the "Critical Theories for Liturgical Theology" seminar. Their ongoing guidance and feedback have been invaluable. This book has also benefited from the feedback of family and friends who graciously read and commented on drafts along the way: Dan and Dorothy Turnbloom, Paul Turnbloom,

Fr. George Gray, and Fr. Richard Rutherford. Lastly, to all the friends and family who have patiently and lovingly supported us through the researching and writing of this book. Thank you all for being sources of grace in our lives.

Key Terms

Survivor vs. Victim: Throughout this book we have elected to use the language of *survivor* to describe people who have experienced clergy-perpetrated sexual abuse (CPSA), rather than language like *victim* or *people who have experienced abuse*. While there is no one right or wrong word here, we believe that ultimately it should be up to the person to identify the language that best explains that person's experience. Most of the contemporary research that has informed our work has opted to use the word *survivor*. So, we follow suit for linguistic consistency. It should be noted, however, that not everyone who experiences trauma or CPSA survives. Yet, we have elected to use the word *survivor* in an attempt to center the experience and identity of the survivor rather than the perpetrator, simultaneously emphasizing the resilience of those living through trauma.

Systemic Clergy-Perpetrated Sexual Abuse or Systemic CPSA: We use the term *systemic CPSA* to describe the crisis in which members of the Roman Catholic clergy repeatedly used their position in the Church to abuse others. In response, the institutional church has repeatedly covered up the abuse, refused to report the abuse to legal authorities, and failed to provide justice to those affected. This pattern of systemic negligent behavior was reported on by the *Boston Globe* in 2002, bringing widespread attention to the issue.

Clericalism: A culture that regards and treats priests, bishops, and deacons (clerics) as greater than the lay population. It is a hierarchical system that simultaneously bestows clerics with inflated authoritative power to wield over their communities while diminishing the role of the laity in the Church.

Liturgy: Liturgy is a communal ritual of prayer through which the Church worships God. For example, whenever a congregation gathers as an assembly to celebrate any of the seven sacraments (baptism, confirmation, the Eucharist, penance, anointing of the sick, matrimony, or holy orders) it is celebrating a liturgy. However, there are other liturgies that are not one of the seven sacraments. For instance, the stations of the cross, Good Friday services, the liturgy of the hours, and funerals are all examples of liturgies, even though they are not counted among the seven sacraments. So, whenever Christians gather to pray together, they are participating in the liturgical life of the Church.

Roman Catholic vs. Catholic: When we write *Catholic* throughout this book, we are referring to the Roman Catholic Church. The term *catholic* is sometimes used to describe Eastern Catholic Churches in communion with the Roman Catholic Church or to mean "universal" in reference to the entire ecclesial body of Christ. However, unless otherwise specified, we are using the term *Catholic* to refer to the Roman Catholic Church.

Introduction

> *True love for an oppressor means seeking ways to make him cease his oppression; it means stripping him of a power that he does not know how to use, and that diminishes his own humanity and that of others. . . . If a criminal has harmed me or a loved one, no one can forbid me from demanding justice and ensuring that this person—or anyone else—will not harm me, or others, again. This is entirely just; forgiveness does not forbid it but actually demands it.*
> —Pope Francis, *Fratelli Tutti*, no. 241

When examining the experience of liturgy in the shadows of the Roman Catholic sex-abuse crisis, we must begin by appreciating the power of sacramental grace. Such an experience of the sacraments is illustrated in the testimony of a parish leader from Vermont, Valerie Parzyck. She describes her experience when entering the Church in a time of personal struggle:

> As I entered the chapel, I could feel a palpable shift in the air from the flurry of activity outside to the quietness on the inside. I felt peace from within; my body felt lighter, and the air was easier to breathe. I knew at that moment that I was in the presence of something extraordinary.[1]

---

[1] Valerie Parzyck, "Eucharistic Testimonials," Roman Catholic Diocese of Burlington, November 22, 2023.

Parzyck's account attests to the profound healing that she felt when entering the Church; such holistic experiences are not merely emotional; they are often spiritual and physical as well. When she describes being in "the presence of something extraordinary," we hear the firsthand experience of the liturgy's power to transform worshipers. The physical environment of the Church and the beauty of the liturgy served as a source of grace and as a relief for the pain and fear that she was experiencing. Through the grace of the liturgy, she found it easier to breathe and knew that she was in the healing presence of something sacred.

This book is about the power of the liturgy: its power to heal *and* its power to harm. In these pages we examine the harm done to the laity as a result of systemic clergy-perpetrated sexual abuse (CPSA) and the ongoing violence inflicted upon survivors due to the persistence of clericalist culture. The first and second chapters dive deeper into the contexts that shape the CPSA's effect on the liturgy, including the clericalist culture that perpetuates the crisis. We start in Chapter 1 with an exploration of liturgy and grace, describing liturgy as the source and summit of grace. In essence, liturgy is where we can both find and participate in grace. We aim to provide a foundation and shared understanding of liturgy as we discuss how trauma and clericalist culture can affect the liturgical life of the Church, the primary focus of Chapter 2. In this second chapter we present a framework of the Roman Catholic clericalist culture and examine how it enables systemic CPSA to flourish.

For some survivors of sexual abuse the liturgy has become a space of violence, a stark contrast to the positive experience of the liturgy described by Parzyck. For these individuals the liturgy has become a space that brings immense spiritual, emotional, and, at times, physical pain, effectively halting their ability to experience the liturgy in the same way that Parzyck does. For some survivors of CPSA, participating in the liturgy becomes a violent experience that affects all aspects of their emotional, spiritual, and physical well-being. The third chapter further explores how post-traumatic stress disorder (PTSD) transforms the liturgy into an experience of violence. We discuss the liturgical experiences of CPSA survivors, reflecting upon how their predispositions impact their experience of the liturgy after being abused.

Beyond the PTSD experienced by survivors of systemic CPSA, many members of the Catholic Church report a strong sense of betrayal that negatively affects their participation in the liturgical life of the Church. The fourth and fifth chapters discuss how the Church's institutional betrayal can cause conditions known as moral injury and moral distress, respectively. Feeling betrayed by the Church can lead to both a loss of faith and a feeling of complicity that greatly hinders the power of the liturgy. Marie Collins speaks to the violence that she feels in Catholic liturgical settings despite her abuser's admission of guilt in court. Collins, a survivor of clerical abuse in a hospital setting, expresses her continued struggle to regain trust and faith in her religion. Collins describes the continued process of coping with the failure of the Catholic Church as an institution:

> My one regret is that I can rarely bring myself to practice my Catholic religion. My faith in God has not been touched. I can forgive my abuser for his actions. He has admitted his guilt. But how do I regain my respect for the leadership of my church?[2]

---

[2] Marie Collins and Sheila Hollins, "Healing a Wound at the Heart of the Church and Society," in *Toward Healing and Renewal: The 2012 Symposium on the Sexual Abuse of Minors Held at the Pontifical Gregorian University*,

Collins's testimony emphasizes that it is unfair and unethical to view the survivors who refuse to return to the Church as traitors or in any sense less faithful in their belief in God. Instead, Collins's testimony illustrates the continued harm that the culture within the Catholic Church has had on the lay population. While some survivors found a healing environment in the presence of supportive clergy, others, failed by Church leadership, remain suspicious of the Catholic Church's intentions and continue to experience a lack of grace when participating in the liturgical life of the Church. Within Collins's testimony, we witness an individual continuing to struggle to regain hope in the Church despite direct admissions of guilt from the abuser.

Once we have explored the shadows of trauma—PTSD, moral injury, and moral distress—in the third, fourth, and fifth chapters, we turn our attention to how the clericalist culture of the Church can be uprooted and its impacts healed. In the sixth chapter we examine the Church's theologies of ordained ministry through the lenses of substance and relational ontologies. All too often clergy are seen in a way that reduces their role in the liturgy to interchangeable symbols tasked with dispensing God's grace. This view both overemphasizes clerics, placing them as gatekeepers of salvation, and ironically, limits their role in the Church community. Instead, we argue that the Church should see the authority and liturgical role of ministers as a gift that is given through their relationships with the laity. This way of seeing ordained ministry combats clericalism by rooting clerics' identity in their community, providing greater accountability for themselves and serving their community more fully. In the seventh chapter we focus on a particular

---

ed. Charles J. Scicluna, Hans Zollner, and David John Ayotte (Mahwah, NJ: Paulist Press, 2012), 26.

rhetorical way of describing the liturgy among Catholic officials in their responses to the sexual-abuse crisis. Liturgy is seen and described as an obligation and an exclusive source of salvation that cannot be found outside of the Church. We look at the rhetoric used by Catholic leaders who are responding to the systemic CPSA crisis and how clericalist culture and language around obligation often works to guilt survivors into staying in the Church at the expense of their own mental and spiritual well-being. This rhetoric affects not just survivors, but all members of the Church who are seeking to heal and repair from the institutional failures related to systemic CPSA. We then offer alternative language that avoids retraumatization and aims to empower rather than control the laity.

Finally, in the eighth chapter we explore salvation inside and outside of the Roman Catholic Church. First, we take a closer look into the understanding of salvation as it is described in the documents of the Second Vatican Council, namely, the affirmation of the possibility of salvation outside of the Catholic Church. Then we turn to the dark reality that, for many affected by systemic CPSA, the liturgy is no longer fruitful and, thus, there is no longer salvation *inside* the Church. We conclude that, for some, leaving the Church is necessary for their salvation, and it is our obligation to promote salvation and healing above all else, wherever one may find it.

Throughout this book we focus heavily on the need for cultural reform. There may be a temptation to push back on this critique and locate the problem in the survivor instead. That is, there may be a temptation to treat the Church as perfect as it is, affected by only a few bad actors, placing the onus on the laity to heal, come to terms with the CPSA crisis, and return to the Church to fulfil their holy obligation. Here, it is helpful to quote the work of Hilary Jerome Scarsella, who identifies and summarizes this issue well:

> Some theologians may prefer theories that maintain a concept of the liturgy *in itself* or of a liturgical *essence* that stands apart from its cultural construction and appropriation by ritual participants. This kind of theory, together with a conviction that the essence of the liturgy is good, would likely reason that when ritual participation results in harm, that harm ought to be traced to misinterpretation on the part of the participant and not to the liturgy itself. Such an approach succeeds in protecting the sanctity of religious ritual and posits an explanation for how the harm of sexual abuse is exacerbated through communion participation, but the conclusion that participants who are harmfully impacted by participation in religious ritual suffer merely due to their own misinterpretation is a sophisticated form of victim blaming. It turns survivors' testimony into a weapon wielded to dismiss and invalidate survivors' warnings that something is amiss in the broader practice of communion. In particular, since the harm in question is that of sexualized violence, we must be highly skeptical of any analytical paradigm that locates the source of harm in the one who is being harmed. We need a theoretical framework that traces the harm survivors have incurred to systems and practices that exist outside of survivors themselves.[3]

Scarsella explains that it is not only unhelpful to identify the problem with survivors instead of the culture, but that it is actively harmful. So, while we want to attend to the experiences of survivors and those affected by systemic CPSA, we

---

[3] Hilary Jerome Scarsella, "Victimization via Ritualization: Christian Communion and Sexual Abuse," in *Trauma and Lived Religion: Transcending the Ordinary*, ed. R. Ruard Ganzevoort and Srjdan Sremac (Cham, Switzerland, 2018), 230.

are by no means holding them responsible for their abuse or its consequences. Rather, we argue for lasting cultural reform to bring justice to survivors, victims, and the Church as a whole.

As Pope Francis makes emphatically clear in his encyclical letter *Fratelli Tutti*, Catholics ought to hold wrongdoers and oppressors accountable out of a sense of duty, forgiveness, and love. In this book we are not calling for cultural reform simply to condemn the Church for its actions. It is through the power of the liturgy and the grace it offers that the Church can and must do better. By demanding reform, we answer Pope Francis's call for justice that is rooted in love:

> We are called to love everyone, without exception; at the same time, loving an oppressor does not mean allowing him to keep oppressing us, or letting him think that what he does is acceptable. On the contrary, true love for an oppressor means seeking ways to make him cease his oppression; it means stripping him of a power that he does not know how to use, and that diminishes his own humanity and that of others. Forgiveness does not entail allowing oppressors to keep trampling on their own dignity and that of others, or letting criminals continue their wrongdoing. Those who suffer injustice have to defend strenuously their own rights and those of their family, precisely because they must preserve the dignity they have received as a loving gift from God. If a criminal has harmed me or a loved one, no one can forbid me from demanding justice and ensuring that this person—or anyone else—will not harm me, or others, again. This is entirely just; forgiveness does not forbid it but actually demands it (*FT*, no. 241).

1

Cultivating Grace through Liturgy

> *The sacraments are efficacious signs of grace, instituted by Christ and entrusted to the Church, by which divine life is dispensed to us. The visible rites by which the sacraments are celebrated signify and make present the graces proper to each sacrament. They bear fruit in those who receive them with the required dispositions.*
> —CATECHISM OF THE CATHOLIC CHURCH,
> #1131

> *The liturgy is the summit toward which the activity of the Church is directed; at the same time it is the font from which all her power flows.*
> CONSTITUTION ON THE SACRED LITURGY,
> #10

In December of 1963, Pope Paul VI promulgated the *Constitution on the Sacred Liturgy* (*Sacrosanctum Concilium*), the first of sixteen documents that would be created by the Second Vatican Council. This document was the direct result of decades of pastoral and scholarly work known as the liturgical renewal. The liturgical renewal was an international movement, undertaken by laity, scholars, and clergy, that was intended to reinvigorate the liturgical life of the Church, ultimately culminating in the systematic reform of all facets of the Church's liturgical prayer.[1] While the movement certainly involved many different Christian denominations, the liturgical renewal had a particularly immense influence on the way the Roman Catholic Church celebrated the liturgy.

Central to the Roman Catholic liturgical renewal was the desire to reform and promote the role the liturgy has in the life of the Church. The *Constitution on the Sacred Liturgy* famously emphasized the need for "fully conscious, and active participation in liturgical celebrations" (*SC*, #14). Too often, the laity's experience of the liturgy had become passive and detached. Sitting in the pews silently as the priests prayed quietly in Latin with their backs to the congregation, it became all too easy for the laity to "check out" and let the ministers do the praying. Participation for the laity was often reduced to attending, sitting with reverence, and receiving communion when the time came. Much of the rich language and beautiful symbols contained in the liturgy were either imperceptible or left unnoticed. A poem in a dead language, whispered beneath one's breath, the immense power of the liturgy was undeniably

---

[1] For a history of the liturgical renewal, see Annibale Bugnini, *The Reform of the Liturgy, 1948–1975* (Collegeville, MN: Liturgical Press, 1990); Piero Marini, Mark R. Francis, John R. Page, and Keith F. Pecklers, *A Challenging Reform: Realizing the Vision of the Liturgical Renewal, 1963–1975* (Collegeville, MN: Liturgical Press, 2007); Katharine E. Harmon, *There Were Also Many Women There: Lay Women in the Liturgical Movement in the United States, 1926–59* (Collegeville, MN: Liturgical Press, 2012); Massimo Faggioli, *True Reform: Liturgy and Ecclesiology in* Sacrosanctum Concilium (Collegeville, MN: Liturgical Press, 2012); John F. Baldovin, *Reforming the Liturgy: A Response to the Critics* (Collegeville, MN: Liturgical Press, 2008); Stephanie Perdew, "Fruits of the Liturgical Renewal Movement: Introduction," *Liturgy* 36, no. 3 (2021): 1–4; Nicholas E. Denysenko, *Liturgical Reform after Vatican II: The Impact on Eastern Orthodoxy* (Minneapolis: Fortress Press, 2015).

present but rendered far less effective than it might be, if only the laity could hear, understand, and participate. In short, the liturgical reform was concerned that the relationship between the liturgy and the lives of the lay faithful was being neglected.

So, in the wake of the Second Vatican Council, the Catholic Church engaged in a process of liturgical reform. Guided by *Sacrosanctum Concilium*, the Church translated the liturgy into vernacular languages that allowed people to comprehend more readily the words they were hearing.[2] Many altars were moved away from the walls so that ministers could face the congregations instead of standing with their backs to them. These and many other carefully researched, tested, and implemented reforms were done so that all people, clergy and laity alike, would be more able to participate fully in the liturgical life of the Church.[3] The result was a liturgy that was better able to have a concrete influence on the individual lives of the faithful, the communal life of the Church, and the life of the world that the Church is called to serve.

What Is the Liturgy?

Given the momentous reforms of the liturgical renewal, one of our goals in this chapter is to better understand *Sacrosanctum Concilium*'s vision for a liturgy that brings life to the Church and the world. In essence, we are seeking to answer this question:

---

[2] For a thorough examination of the process of reforming the liturgy for a diversity of cultures, see the work of Anscar J. Chupungco, *Cultural Adaptation of the Liturgy* (New York: Paulist Press, 1982); Anscar J. Chupungco, *Liturgies of the Future: The Process and Methods of Inculturation* (New York: Paulist Press, 1989); Anscar J. Chupungco, *Liturgical Inculturation: Sacramentals, Religiosity, and Catechesis* (Collegeville, MN: Liturgical Press, 1992); Anscar J. Chupungco, *What Then, Is Liturgy? Musings and Memoir* (Collegeville, MN: Liturgical Press, 2010).

[3] Marini, Francis, Page, and Pecklers, *A Challenging Reform*.

What is the liturgy? What does it mean to participate in the liturgy? And, finally, what does it mean to say that the liturgy is the source and summit of the Church's life? Another way of asking these questions is simply to ask, What does it mean for the liturgy to work? To begin answering these questions, we first describe what the Roman Catholic tradition means by the word *liturgy*.

First, *liturgy is a communal ritual of prayer* through which the Church worships God. For example, whenever a congregation gathers as an assembly to celebrate any of the seven sacraments (that is, baptism, confirmation, Eucharist, penance, anointing of the sick, matrimony, or holy orders) they are celebrating a liturgy. However, there are other liturgies as well. For instance, the stations of the cross, Good Friday services, the liturgy of the hours, and funerals are all examples of liturgies even though they are not counted among the seven sacraments. So, whenever Christians gather to pray together, they are engaging in liturgy.

For example, for many families holiday meals play a particularly important role in bringing the family members together and creating their unique bond as a family. Special holidays like birthdays, anniversaries, and New Year's celebrations bring the family together in a particularly beautiful and powerful way. However, although they are often seen as less important, the lunches a family has on regular Saturdays, or the breakfasts they hurriedly share on their way to work and school, are also important for shaping the identity of the family. Just because a meal doesn't seem particularly special doesn't mean that it isn't important and powerful. The same is true of liturgies. Just because a liturgy isn't one of the seven sacraments does not mean that it has no impact on the life of the Church community. Throughout this book, whenever we use the term *the liturgy*, we are referring to the entire liturgical life of the Church, the sum total of the many diverse liturgical rituals celebrated by the Church.

Second, *liturgies are rituals that engage the bodies and senses of the worshipers.* The liturgy is not limited to spoken language. Rather, liturgies are made up of many different types of symbols. In addition to spoken words, liturgical prayer may also include symbols such as architecture, artwork, music, gestures, touch, vestments, incense, food, oil, and water. In other words, liturgy is made up of symbols that engage all of our senses. For example, restaurant owners pay special attention to ambiance, because they know that a diner's experience is heavily influenced by things such as the choice of music being played, the artwork on the walls, the lighting on the tables, the uniforms worn by the waitstaff, and the beauty of the dishes and cutlery. Making a diner feel welcome and cared for is much more than a matter of saying, "Welcome!" Humans relate to our surroundings using all of our senses. The same is true of liturgical prayer. Hence, St. Augustine of Hippo famously referred to some aspects of the liturgy as "visible words."[4] When communities celebrate liturgies, they taste the sweetness of wine, they feel the coolness of water, they smell the sweetness of balsam, they see the radiance of light through stained glass, and they hear the rhythm of solemn chanting. Liturgy is not merely a verbal and intellectual exercise that ignores the fact that humans are essentially embodied creatures.[5]

Third, *liturgy provides a personal encounter with Jesus.* According to the Roman Catholic tradition, Jesus is made truly present through the celebration of the liturgy. As Jesus says in the Gospel of Matthew, "For where two or three are gathered in my name, I am there among them" (Mt 18:20). According

---

[4] See Augustine of Hippo, *Against Faustus the Manichean*, 19.16.

[5] Frank C. Senn, *Embodied Liturgy: Lessons in Christian Ritual* (Minneapolis: Fortress Press, 2016).

to *Sacrosanctum Concilium*, "Christ is always present in His Church, especially in her liturgical celebrations" (*SC*, #7). However, importantly, no liturgical celebration is enough to encapsulate and exhaust the presence of Jesus. Because Jesus Christ is a Mystery that transcends human understanding, it is impossible for any single liturgical celebration to exhaust the presence of Christ.[6]

To put this in perspective, when we first begin a relationship with a friend, we might spend a good amount of time getting to know them by sharing a meal or a coffee at a shop. However, if we want to develop a truly intimate and meaningful relationship with that person, we need to encounter them through other settings and interactions. We might visit them at work; celebrate birthdays with them; go to the movies; comfort one another during difficult moments; help them move into a new home, and so on. The first time we meet them at the coffee shop, they are undeniably present as we begin to know one another. In and through the diversity of all these other encounters, we begin to discover the inexhaustible depths of who they are. The same is true of Jesus's presence in the liturgy. The rich diversity of the symbols that have been woven together by the various liturgical traditions all work together to provide a deep, ongoing relationship of personal encounter with the risen Jesus Christ that unfolds over a lifetime of participating in the liturgy.

Fourth, because it provides a personal encounter with Jesus, *the liturgy sanctifies the Church and the world*. The fourth-century bishop and theologian St. Athanasius of Alexandria writes that "the Son of God became man so that we might

---

[6] *Catechism of the Catholic Church, Second Edition, Revised in Accordance with the Official Latin Text Promulgated by Pope John Paul II* (Vatican City: Libreria Editrice Vaticana, 1997), #1201.

become God."[7] In other words, the purpose of Jesus's presence in the world is to make the world more like him. This process is known as divinization or *theosis*. Salvation is a process of becoming more like God. It is not enough to be amazed that Jesus is present, simply basking in his close proximity. Christians are called to *respond* by changing their lives to be more like Jesus, so that they, in turn, become the presence of Jesus to the world. Or, to use a familiar poem:

> Christ has no body but yours,
> No hands, no feet on earth but yours,
> Yours are the eyes with which He looks
> Compassion on this world,
> Yours are the feet with which He walks to
>   do good,
> Yours are the hands, with which He blesses
>   all the world.[8]

The presence of Jesus in the liturgy makes the Church holy when it increases and directs the way that Christians actively love God, one another, and the world. When the Church celebrates the liturgy, it is opening itself up to Jesus's presence so that it might better strive to become more like Jesus. Called to be the body of Christ (1 Cor 12; Rom 2; Eph 1; Col 1), Christian disciples are a community that is tasked with becoming more like Jesus in order to make Jesus present to the world.

What does it mean to participate in the liturgy? When we consider this question, we specifically want to describe what it means to fully, consciously, and actively participate in the

---

[7] Athanasius, *On the Incarnation*, trans. John Behr (Crestwood, NY: St. Vladimir's Seminary Press, 2012), 201, #54.

[8] For an examination of this poem's authorship, see Timothy Phillips, "Whose Hands? Another Possible Case of Cumulative Authorship," *Mockingbird's Imitations* (blog), November 7, 2011.

liturgy.⁹ As we mentioned above, *Sacrosanctum Concilium* set out a clear goal to reinvigorate the way that Roman Catholics celebrated the liturgy. *Sacrosanctum Concilium* encourages pastors to seek more than mere attendance from the laity:

> Pastors of souls must therefore realize that, when the liturgy is celebrated, something more is required than the mere observation of the laws governing valid and licit celebration; it is their duty also to ensure that the faithful take part fully aware of what they are doing, actively engaged in the rite, and enriched by its effects. (*SC*, #11)

As we will address in greater detail in the following section, it can be common for pastors to be preoccupied with simply performing the liturgy exactly as it is prescribed in the official ritual texts (rubrics) that have been written by Church authorities. The words *valid* and *licit* are used in the above passage to indicate that a liturgy has been celebrated in accordance with the current rubrics. Preoccupation with validity can occur for many reasons, some better than others. However, it often results in the pastor ignoring the role of the laity in the liturgical celebration. When this happens, participation is reduced to passive attendance. At its worst, preoccupation with validity ends up making pastors see lay participation as a nuisance (perhaps even a threat) that can get in the way of celebrating the liturgy.

For example, a professor might spend a great deal of time planning a lesson for their students. They create a PowerPoint

---

⁹ Since the publication of the *Constitution on the Sacred Liturgy*, there has been a wealth of commentary on how one should understand the phrase "full, conscious, and active participation." Taylor W. Burton-Edwards, "Perspectives and Limitations of Current Theories in Neuroscience and Cosmology in Describing 'Full, Conscious and Actual Participation in Liturgical Celebrations,'" *Liturgy* 28, no. 4 (2013): 41–59.

presentation with a clear order, and they design activities that will help the students better understand the concepts being taught. However, when the students arrive, they are different than the professor expected them to be. One student couldn't get a babysitter for their toddler (who is now wandering around the classroom). Another student is dealing with a great deal of stress from an argument with their partner. Another student arrives with accommodations for a hearing impairment. When the lesson begins, the students struggle to pay attention, and they ask questions that go off on tangents. Despite the professor's best efforts, the original lesson plan is not coming to fruition. It could be easy for this teacher to feel like their lesson has been ruined by these students. However, a wise and experienced teacher will find ways to adjust (often chaotically and in the moment) to the differences among the students who arrive in their classroom. Instead of seeing these students as bringing weaknesses that threaten the lesson, a good teacher knows how to see these differences as strengths to be acknowledged and utilized in the classroom. Put differently, good teachers know that the work of education is a collaboration with the students. Any lesson plan that doesn't consider how the students will use their unique gifts to contribute to one another's education has fundamentally misunderstood the nature of learning. So it is with the laity's full, conscious, and active participation in the liturgy.

Worshipers need to be seen as collaborators whose active engagement with the diverse symbols of the liturgy is a necessary component of the liturgy's success. It is not acceptable to expect each worshiper to behave in the same, passive manner during the celebration of the liturgy. As St. Paul emphasized in his first letter to the Corinthians, every worshiper has a unique contribution to make to the liturgy (1 Cor 14:26). The mark of a truly gifted pastor is the ability to guide these contributions in a way that manifests a liturgy that builds up the life of the Church.

Bearing this vision of liturgical participation in mind, we turn our attention to this question: What does it mean to say that the liturgy is simultaneously the source and the summit of the Church's divine life? In the words of *Sacrosanctum Concilium*, "The liturgy is the summit toward which the activity of the Church is directed; at the same time it is the font [or source] from which all her power flows" (*SC*, #10). First, the liturgy is said to be the *source* of the Church's divine life because Jesus is truly present in and encountered through the symbols of the liturgy. Or, to use the language of *Sacrosanctum Concilium*, the liturgy "draws the faithful into the compelling love of Christ and sets them on fire" (*SC*, #10). As we noted earlier, the liturgy provides a personal encounter with Jesus that is aimed at transforming the members of the Church more fully into the presence of Jesus. Through the liturgy the Church is invited to share in the gift of Jesus's divine life. *Grace* is another common word for "sharing in the divine life of Christ." According to the thirteenth-century Dominican friar and doctor of the Church, St. Thomas Aquinas, "Grace is nothing else than a participated likeness of the Divine Nature."[10] In other words, grace is a way of sharing in Jesus's life that makes us more like Jesus. When the Church has a personal encounter with Jesus in and through the liturgy, they are being offered the opportunity to participate in the grace of Christ. Hence, the liturgy is rightly called a source of grace for the Church.

Second, the liturgy is described as the *summit* of the Church's life. Liturgy, then, is the summit of the Christian way of life because it is the "means whereby the faithful may express in their lives, and manifest to others, the mystery of

---

[10] Thomas Aquinas, *Summa Theologiae*, III.62.1c.

Christ" (*SC*, #2). When Roman Catholics gather together and celebrate the liturgy, the liturgy becomes a powerful moment when the unique contributions of community members work together to manifest their shared identity as the body of Christ. This does not mean that the Church is *only* the body of Christ when celebrating the liturgy. For example, a soccer team most fully manifests its shared identity as a *team* when it plays (and hopefully wins) a soccer match. That match is its primary reason for existing. However, everything that happens in between soccer matches is still a crucial part of their identity as a team. Each player has their own unique community that helps them through their struggles. When the goal keepers gather with their coach, they are bonding and forming special skills that will allow them to play their role during the match. When the team travels together for away games, they are building relationships that influence how they will play as a team. All of these activities (and many more) are necessary parts of who they are as a team. However, when the whistle blows to begin a match, all of those other activities find their fullest fruition. The match is the summit of a soccer team's life. The same is true of the liturgy for the Church. The daily lives of Christians (for example, their families, their jobs, their friendships, their hobbies, their work for justice, and so on) are all essential to the identity of the Church. But Christian lives reach their fullest expression when all those unique activities are brought together in full, conscious, and active participation in the liturgy. In those moments the Church is most fully the body of Christ. In celebrating the liturgy, the Church becomes the fullness of grace.

So, what does it mean for the liturgy to work? In essence, the liturgy works when it is *both* the source *and* summit of grace. The liturgy works when it provides a personal encounter with Christ, offering grace to those who gather. The liturgy works when it transforms the lives of worshipers in a way that leads them to live lives animated by the faith, hope, and love of Christ. Simultaneously, the liturgy works when it provides an opportunity for the Church members to gather together, offering praise and thanksgiving to God for the divine life they have been given. These initial thoughts regarding the nature of the liturgy and its relationship to grace prepare us to consider two ways of conceptualizing the liturgy that can either support or confound the liturgy's ability to realize its dual purpose of being *both* the source *and* summit of grace.

Liturgy Dispensing Grace

According to the *Catechism of the Catholic Church,* "The sacraments are efficacious signs of grace, instituted by Christ and entrusted to the Church, by which divine life is dispensed to us."[11] In its original Latin, the word that is translated into English as "dispensed" is the word *praebetur*. In most of the other instances that the word *praebetur* appears in the *Catechism*, it is translated into English as "offered." So, the translators could have rendered this sentence as "by which divine life is offered to us." In this and the following section we present two different ways of imagining the relationship between the liturgy and grace. On one hand, the liturgy can be seen as a ritual process that *dispenses* grace. From this perspective grace is easily imagined as a substance (that is, sacred stuff) that is produced by the liturgy. On the other hand, the liturgy can be imagined as a ritual form of divine communication whereby God *offers* grace. From this perspective, grace is imagined as a provocative task to be accepted, a way of life to be lived. The next section of this chapter examines what it means to say that liturgy *offers*

---

[11] *Catechism of the Catholic Church,* #1131.

grace. In the present section we focus on the risks inherent in seeing liturgy as a process of *dispensing* grace. In short, if the liturgy is primarily imagined as dispensing grace, two harmful consequences can arise. First, the liturgy is seen only as a source of grace. Second, the role of the ordained ministers is overemphasized. These consequences make it difficult for the liturgy to accomplish its goal. A liturgy that is seen as a tool for dispensing grace is a liturgy that will struggle to work.

One of the primary ways that the Roman Catholic tradition has described the relationship between the liturgy and grace has been to imagine the liturgy as a series of rituals that produce grace in the way a factory assembly line produces a product. Put differently, the liturgy is described as a process of mechanistic production. If the right person says the right words while using the right materials, then the automatic and inevitable result is grace being dispensed to the laity. When seen this way, it is easy to think that the liturgy exists to create a commodity (that is, valuable stuff) that is then handed out to the faithful by uniquely skilled "factory workers" known as clergy. In essence, by translating *praebetur* as "dispensed," the translators of the *Catechism* make it easy to imagine grace as a commodified substance and the clergy as powerful gatekeepers of that substance. Grace is produced by clergy through the liturgy, and dispensed to those who passively witness the rituals. Translating *praebetur* as "dispensed" strongly implies that grace is not an activity, but something produced and allocated to passive participants.

This way of understanding liturgical efficacy finds its roots in a misuse of St. Augustine of Hippo's famous phrase: *ex opere operato*. This Latin expression, often translated as "from the work having been worked," was used by Augustine in the fifth century to argue that the sacraments are efficacious (that is, they work) when they are validly performed. According to

Augustine, when an ordained minister performs the liturgy the way it is prescribed, it works because it was carried out as the Church intended it to be performed. Augustine used the concept *ex opere operato* to argue against the Donatists, a sect of Christians who claimed that sacraments performed by immoral ministers were invalid and needed to be redone by moral ministers.[12] Due to persecution from Emperor Diocletian in the fourth century, some ministers renounced their faith and handed the sacred scriptures over to their persecutors. These ministers became known as apostates and traitors. The Donatists claimed that any baptism performed by these ministers was invalid because of the ministers' immorality. Augustine argued, to the contrary, that these baptisms were valid and did not need to be redone. Because Jesus is present and active in the liturgy, the moral quality (whether immoral or saintly) of a particular minister does not affect the validity of liturgies they perform. Rather, the liturgy is valid and "works" because of Christ's presence. In other words, the concept of *ex opere operato* protects the validity of the liturgy by declaring that grace is not dependent on the moral quality of the minister who is performing the sacrament or on the person receiving the grace. To connect this to the context of the Catholic sex-abuse crisis, Augustine would argue that a liturgy can still be valid even if it is performed by an abusive priest or a bishop who has covered up abuse. In short, the concept of *ex opere operato* protects the liturgy from corruption and affirms the presence of grace even when an immoral member of the clergy is presiding. In this way the liturgy is primarily seen as a prescribed ritual with power

---

[12] For an in-depth discussion of the Donatist controversy, see Adam D. Ployd, "The Power of Baptism: Augustine's Pro-Nicene Response to the Donatists," *Journal of Early Christian Studies* 22, no. 4 (2014): 519–40.

that transcends its particular context. Just because a liturgy is performed by an apostate or an abusive priest does not mean that it is an invalid source of grace.

Since Augustine's writings against the Donatists, Roman Catholic sacramental theology has placed an immense amount of emphasis on the relationship between the source of grace (Jesus) and the instrument of grace (the liturgy). This emphasis allows grace to be imagined as a product that is dispensed. Valid liturgies are seen to cause an effect in the world regardless of the context in which they are celebrated. This means that the particular status of the recipient or the moral standing of the minister play no role in the mechanistic production of grace. As such, care for liturgy primarily means care for rubrics; the validity of the liturgy becomes the priority.

Pointing out the dangers of focusing on liturgical validity, sacramental theologian Peter Fink argues:

> It is probably the case that the sharp line drawn between valid and invalid is no longer the most helpful way to assess the truth or untruth of the sacraments. Both are minimalist judgements: either the essentials are there or not . . . even where the essentials are judged not to be present [that is, the sacrament is invalid], it is difficult to dismiss the act as empty and without sacramental value; defective, perhaps, but not without value.[13]

Nor is it insufficient for achieving full efficacy. It is not that validity lacks importance, but it is not the end-all-and-be-all of liturgy. An overly narrow focus on validity ignores important concerns about efficacy. For Fink, an invalid liturgy can still

---

[13] Peter E. Fink, *The New Dictionary of Sacramental Worship* (Collegeville, MN: Liturgical Press, 1990), 1299.

have meaning and value. It can still work. We will return to this point in the following section, but here suffice it to say that a preoccupation with validity can allow a minister to forget that the liturgy's primary purpose is to transform the lives of the faithful, making them more like Christ. Essentially, preoccupation with validity allows one to mistake the means for the end.

In addition to seeing grace as a substance that is produced by a valid liturgy, one of the great dangers of imagining the liturgy as a ritual that dispenses grace is an overemphasis on the indispensability of the ordained minister. By focusing so narrowly on the liturgy as the source of grace, the cleric who is performing the liturgical ritual is afforded a dangerous amount of power. Within this mechanistic view of the liturgy, there is a great deal of emphasis on the minister; "acting in the person of Christ, he makes present the Eucharistic sacrifice, and offers it to God in the name of all the people" (*Lumen Gentium*, #10). When we overemphasize the liturgy as the source of grace, it is inevitable that the minister's authority and identity as Christ will eclipse the other forms of Christ's presence in the liturgy. If only his actions can produce the grace that then gets dispensed, he becomes a gatekeeper to salvation and a member of a holier (and higher) caste. One word that is often used to describe this dangerous power imbalance is *clericalism*.

Clericalism creates an ideal environment for abusive power to take control over the laity. Its unique structures create a caste system of superior men who enjoy an all-too-easily abused divine authority. Or, in the words of David Clohessy, the director of the Survivors Network of those Abused by Priests (SNAP),

> For centuries the (Catholic) Church hierarchy has been a rigid, secretive, all male monarchy and remains so today; that is the crux of the crisis right there.... With virtually no checks and balances, you have almost limitless

power in the hands of a few secretive men. That alone is a recipe for disaster.[14]

This contradicts the need to see liturgical participation as openness to collaboration with others. Viewing lay participation as fundamentally passive creates the pathway for objectification and control.[15] A liturgy that dispenses grace is a liturgy that prioritizes the power of the clergy. A liturgy that dispenses grace is a liturgy that serves clericalism.

Despite the prevalence of this dangerous way of imagining the liturgy, there have always been alternative frameworks provided by Roman Catholic tradition. This clericalist approach to the liturgy can be avoided by choosing instead to see the liturgy as a participative encounter with Jesus and an invitation into God's life. Put differently, our fundamental way of looking at liturgy should be as a sacred activity through which grace is not *dispensed*, but *offered* to the participants.

Liturgy Offering Grace

Having laid out the dangers that arise from seeing the liturgy as a process of *dispensing* grace, we can turn our attention to the benefits of seeing the liturgy as a process of *offering* grace. In essence, when we see the liturgy as a process of offering grace, we maintain a view of the liturgy as both the source *and* the summit of grace. Instead of viewing the liturgy as a process of grace production, the liturgy is instead seen as a process of grace communication. When understood as a pro-

---

[14] Ashamed M. Muhammad, "Catholic Church Accused of Denying Justice to Blacks Abused by Priests," *The Final Call*, December 8, 2009.

[15] In later chapters we return to a discussion of how clericalism perpetuates a culture of control and objectification in ways that are strikingly similar to the way that domestic abusers objectify and control their victims.

cess of offering grace, the liturgy's symbols are seen as God's loving and provocative communication to a people who are called to respond.

In order to understand what it means to say that the liturgy offers grace, we might say that the liturgy is the source of grace in the way that words are a source of friendship. Speaking does not even ensure comprehension, much less ensure a friendship. Words are not mechanisms that guarantee the production of friendship. And yet it is impossible to conceive of a friendship that completely lacks communication. Words are necessary but not sufficient for the creation of a friendship. Communication is the means by which one might offer friendship to another, but it takes a response from the listener if a friendship is to occur. The same is true of the liturgy and grace.

As we discussed earlier in this chapter, the liturgy is made up of many symbols. Some of those symbols are verbal words and some are visible words that engage the bodies of the worshipers. Together, all of those symbols communicate God's presence to the worshiper, providing a personal encounter. When one of our friends smiles at us, hugs us, and tells us that we are loved, that friend's presence is made real and effective through the smile, the hug, and the words "I love you." And yet, friendship is a two-way process. If I cannot understand the meaning behind the smile, the hug, and the words, then my friend's love, while undeniably real and present, is unrequited. Their friendship is offered but not received and not fruitful. Or, to paraphrase the language of the *Catechism*, words of friendship bear fruit in those who receive them with the proper dispositions.[16] When we learn to smile back, hug back, and express our love to our friend, then we have truly received the gift of their friendship. Similarly, when the symbols of the liturgy, which are a symbolic expression of God's love for us,

---

[16] *Catechism of the Catholic Church*, #1131.

also become a symbolic expression of our love for God, this means that we have learned to accept and embody the grace of friendship that God offers through the liturgy.[17] To use the language of Louis-Marie Chauvet, the offer of grace is verified (that is, confirmed and fulfilled) when it is received and returned. In those moments the liturgy has become both the source *and* the summit of God's grace. Just as one cannot be a purely passive recipient of friendship, one cannot be a purely passive recipient of God's grace if that grace is to grow, bear fruit, and enrich our lives. It is, however, important to note that, unlike many human offers of friendship, God's offer of friendship in the liturgy is not revoked if and when it goes unrecognized or unrequited. Through the liturgy, God's offer of grace is unconditional and constant. Just because it is not received immediately, does not mean it cannot be received in time. Like a Shakespearian sonnet that is memorized by a high-school student, it may be experienced at first as nothing more than annoying and confusing sounds with rhythm and rhyme. But, as that student matures over the years, that poem begins to blossom and find meaning within their life. Of course, a good teacher will do everything in their power to help a student understand it at the moment. But, even if they cannot be immediately successful, that does not necessarily mean that the lesson was meaningless.

Understanding the liturgy as an offering of grace implies a necessary concern for the worshiper and their disposition.

---

[17] Here we relate to Chauvet's concept of symbolic exchange. The gift and the return-gift simultaneously constitute a moment of personal encounter. In Benjamin Durheim's words: "The symbol bears a whom who is to be recognized by the recipient. Both the sign and the symbol are given from someone to someone else, but in exchanging a sign it is the what that matters; in giving a symbol what matters is the who who is given to whom." Benjamin Durheim, "Symbolic Exchange and the Gift: Louis-Marie Chauvet and Jacques Derrida in Dialogue," *Obsculta* 4, no. 1 (2011): 41–48.

How are they experiencing the liturgical symbols? Can they understand what the symbols are intended to communicate? Is the communication compelling and effective? In other words, does the worshiper receive the liturgy with the proper disposition for the liturgy to be fruitful? Is the worshiper at a place in their life that allows them to experience the liturgy as an offering of God's loving friendship? These questions are preoccupied with the worshiper and the unique way that they are experiencing the liturgy. Like the good professor in our previous example, a good liturgist's *primary* concern is not performing the liturgy validly, with perfect adherence to the rubrics (although that should be a concern and something taken into deep consideration). Rather, their primary concern should be with communicating God's love to the particular people in their congregation. Again, *Sacrosanctum Concilium* emphasizes as much:

> Something more is required than the mere observation of the laws governing valid and licit celebration; it is [the pastor's] duty also to ensure that the faithful take part fully aware of what they are doing, actively engaged in the rite, and enriched by its effects. (*SC*, #11)

The primary concern for full participation that comes from seeing the liturgy as offering grace allows one to say that validity is not necessary for grace to be offered. Put differently, invalidity does not stop the liturgy from communicating God's grace. As Fink points out, liturgies that fall short of the current magisterial definition of validity do not necessarily lack the ability to communicate grace in an effective manner; these invalid liturgies are not lacking in salvific value. Serving in his role as the prefect of the Congregation for the Doctrine of Faith, Joseph Cardinal Ratzinger forcefully made a similar point in a 1993 letter to Bavarian Lutheran Bishop Johannes Hanselmann. In his letter the future pontiff emphatically affirms the efficacy of "invalid" sacraments:

> I count among the most important results of the ecumenical dialogues the insight that the issue of the eucharist cannot be narrowed to the problem of "validity." Even a theology oriented to the concept of [apostolic] succession, such as that which holds in the Catholic and Orthodox church, should in no way deny the saving presence of the Lord in a Lutheran Lord's Supper.[18]

The invalidity of a liturgy does not mean that it cannot cause grace, just as a misspelled word can still lead to understanding. In fact, what appears as a misspelled word to one culture can be the correct spelling to another culture. While they cannot be separated, any good rhetorician knows that you should not allow the medium to obfuscate the message. By focusing on the liturgy as offering grace, we avoid falling into the trap of overemphasizing the liturgy as the source of grace in a manner that allows us to forget the worshipers. When the worshipers' particular gifts and needs are taken into careful consideration, then the liturgy is not reduced to dispensing a product but is, rather, allowed to communicate a provocative encounter with God's love.

Grace, then, is a way of life into which we are invited. Grace is received as a task to be embraced and fulfilled.[19] The grace

---

[18] Joseph Ratzinger, "Exchange of Letters between Provincial Bishop Johannes Hanselmann and Joseph Cardinal Ratzinger," in *Pilgrim Fellowship of Faith: The Church as Communion* (San Francisco: Ignatius Press, 2005), 91.

[19] Louis-Marie Chauvet, *The Sacraments: The Word of God at the Mercy of the Body*, trans. Madeleine Beaumont (Collegeville, MN: Liturgical Press, 2001), 65.

offered in the liturgy is not a shallow platitude merely stating that God loves us just the way we are, requiring nothing of us. While that is true, it is not the whole story. Rather, the liturgy is a call to action, a vocation. In short, the liturgy requires the full and active participation of the worshipers. As such, it is both the source and summit of the divine life of the Church.

Viewing the liturgy as a ritual that offers grace can help mitigate the clericalism we mentioned above. Shifting the primary focus from validity, which is the purview of the ordained minister, to the fruitful communication of grace decenters the role of the minister. Instead of the gatekeeping authority figure who (both literally and figuratively) stands above the laity, the minister is an indispensable servant who facilitates the conversation occurring between God and the congregation. Because seeing the liturgy as an offering of grace decentralizes ministerial authority, it subverts clericalism and its abuses of ministerial authority. Ministers are not powerful magicians who control God's gifts, dispensing them to the congregation. Even when they preside over a perfectly valid liturgy, they have not fulfilled their mission. The full, active, and conscious participation of the congregation must be the *primary* (but by no means the only) concern of the ordained minister. Viewing grace as a way of life that is being offered rather than a commodity that is being dispensed demands greater care for and involvement of the unique worshipers whom God is calling.

Conclusion: Cultivating Grace through Liturgy

Our goal in this chapter has been to show that the liturgy works when it is both the source and summit of grace. The liturgy works when it forms the Church to live more fully in the love of God. As Pope Pius XII wrote in his 1947 encyclical

Mediator Dei, "The chief element of divine worship must be interior" (*MD*, #24). By this, the pope means that the primary purpose of the liturgy is the interior conversion of the worshipers. All of the symbols that make up the liturgy are meant to serve the transformation of the people participating in the liturgy. Hence, Pius XII encourages the Church to place a strong emphasis on the effects that the liturgy has on the faithful:

> Exterior worship, finally, reveals and emphasizes the unity of the mystical body [that is, the Church], feeds new fuel to its holy zeal, fortifies its energy, intensifies its action day by day: "for although the ceremonies themselves can claim no perfection or sanctity in their own right, they are, nevertheless, the outward acts of religion, designed to rouse the heart, like signals of a sort, to veneration of the sacred realities, and to raise the mind to meditation on the supernatural. They serve to foster piety, to kindle the flame of charity, to increase our faith and deepen our devotion." (*MD*, #23)

Here, Pius XII uses striking language to make the point that the liturgy is a ritual process meant to cultivate grace in the life of the Church. Liturgical rituals are tools used by God to provoke, rouse, foster, and increase the loving friendship of God in the daily lives of the faithful. Exterior worship (that is, the symbols that make up the liturgy) is indispensable, just as communication is indispensable to friendship. However, if we truly care about the liturgy, we must prioritize the people who are called to participate in the liturgy. As the passage from *Sacrosanctum Concilium* reminds us, we must care about the unique dispositions that they bring to the liturgy precisely because those dispositions will determine whether or not the liturgy bears fruit, bringing them more deeply into God's loving friendship.

Caring about the dispositions of those who participate in the liturgy means that we must take into consideration the greater contexts that influence the worshipers' experience of the liturgy. The rest of this book examines how the scandal of systemic clergy perpetrated sexual abuse (CPSA) has inflicted a pervasive trauma on the Church in a manner that corrupts the dispositions necessary for liturgical efficacy. In the current chapter, we have argued that the disposition of the worshipers deserves attention. In order to better understand the effects that systemic CPSA has had on the disposition of those participating in the liturgy, our next chapter provides a sustained look at how clericalism has fueled the abusive culture that allows for the ongoing scandal of systemic CPSA. Further, we describe the traumatic context that has severely disrupted the dispositions necessary for the liturgy to cultivate grace.

The liturgical life of the Church is intended to be a process of cultivating grace. In the liturgy the Church is meant to encounter Christ as one who provocatively calls to us as friends. Instead of viewing grace as a substance that simply can be dispensed and received, we must recognize that grace is an activity that arises from full, conscious, and active participation in the liturgy. However, like all communication offered from one friend to another, liturgical symbols will be experienced differently by people with different dispositions. As we argue, trauma changes the meaning of symbols. In such contexts the liturgy ought not to be expected to work simply because it is validly celebrated. Cultivating grace must become a process of healing that takes the pain and trauma of the worshipers seriously. Without such care, the grace offered by the liturgy becomes ineffective, and the liturgy reaches a state where it is no longer able to serve as the source and the summit of God's loving grace. The Church must strive to be a *source* of grace: an encounter for worshipers to feel loved by God. Additionally, the Church must strive to be a *summit* of grace: empowering worshipers to embody the grace of God in their lives and the lives of others.

2

A Perversion of Power

Understanding Clericalist Culture

> *Clericalism arises from an elitist and exclusivist vision of vocation that interprets the ministry received as a power to be exercised rather than as a free and generous service to be given. This leads us to believe that we belong to a group that has all the answers and no longer needs to listen or learn anything, or that pretends to listen. Clericalism is a perversion and is the root of many evils in the Church: we must humbly ask forgiveness for this and above all create the conditions so that it is not repeated.*
>
> —POPE FRANCIS[1]

In 2018, in the wake of yet another report detailing the breadth and depth of systemic clergy perpetrated sexual-abuse (CPSA), Pope Francis released a "Letter to the People of God" in an attempt to address the gravity of the revelations. In his letter, Pope Francis used a phrase that had been used often by

---

[1] Pope Francis, "Address by His Holiness Pope Francis at the Opening of the Synod of Bishops on Young People, the Faith and Vocational Discernment," October 2018.

Pope John Paul II: "a culture of death." In his 1995 encyclical *Evangelium Vitae*, Pope John Paul II used this phrase to describe a culture that had lost sight of God and, therefore, lost sight of human dignity (*EV*, #21). The result is a deeply secular culture that idolizes individual freedom, glorifying the strong at the expense of the weak and most vulnerable (for example, the unborn, the elderly, the sick, and so on). For John Paul II, a culture of death is a secular culture that is willing to discard human lives to protect its own power and freedom.

In his "Letter to the People of God" Pope Francis uses the phrase "a culture of death," however, to describe a Roman Catholic culture that idolizes itself and is willing to discard human lives to protect its own power and freedom. The importance of Pope Francis's use of the phrase "a culture of death" to describe the pervasive and persistent presence of clericalism in the Roman Catholic Church is that he is asking the Church to take a long look at the plank in their own eye (Mt 7:3). Too often, Roman Catholics are eager to blame the world's moral failures on the specter of secularism that is imagined to be carried out by atheists who despise religion. When Pope Francis describes the culture of the Roman Catholic Church as a culture of death, he is rightly refusing to distract his listeners from the Church's moral and criminal failures; he is refusing to scapegoat others in order to maintain the Church's public image.

The crisis is not the result of a few bad apples who were corrupted by the sexual immorality of the secular world. Rather, Catholic leaders and the Church's clericalist culture are the primary sources of the sexual-abuse crisis. In his letter Pope Francis states, "No effort must be spared to create a culture able to prevent such situations from happening." If such a shift in Roman Catholic clericalist culture (that is, from death to life) is to occur, then the Church must begin with an honest appraisal of structures of sin (to borrow another phrase from John Paul II) that are currently at work in Roman Catholic culture. This chapter examines the culture of death commonly known as clericalism. We offer a brief account of the ways that clericalism has served as the foundation for systemic CPSA to occur. Our goal is to describe how clericalism has inflicted a variety of forms of abuse, leaving in its wake a Church deeply suffering from the consequences of trauma.

Although news of the CPSA scandal peaked in the early 2000s, much of the sexual abuse that was uncovered occurred decades prior. While this has been a talking point often used in an attempt to discredit the prosecution of CPSA cases, the stark decades of silence harken to the true depth of the cultural crisis within the Catholic Church. As noted in various reports from Catholic and secular sources, the ratio of pedophilia displayed by Catholic priests is proportionate to the national rates of abuse.[2] This statistic, while supporting the notion that it is not the identity of a person as a Catholic priest that is directly related to pedophilia, fails to satisfy the feelings of betrayal and confusion that many Catholics feel when confronted with reports of abuse *and* the subsequent cover-ups.

As the breadth of the crisis continued to unfurl in the flurry of lawsuits filed by individuals who had experienced abuse at the hands of priests, members of the laity began asking the question, "How could this happen in our church?" While discussions addressing child abuse began to gain traction in the 1970s, it was not a phenomenon that Catholics expected to

---

[2] John Jay College of Criminal Justice and United States Conference of Catholic Bishops, "The Nature and Scope of Sexual Abuse of Minors by Catholic Priests and Deacons in the United States, 2002: A Research Study Conducted by The John Jay College of Criminal Justice, The City University of New York: For The United States Conference of Catholic Bishops," (Washington, DC: United States Conference of Catholic Bishops, 2004).

occur within their parishes. In addition to grappling with the reality that predatory priests were sexually assaulting children, Catholics were also made aware of the fact that the highest ranking officials in the Church had been aware of these crimes and conspired to conceal them from the public. In order to better protect their reputations, one of the tactics that bishops used to protect the abusers was relocating them to parishes where they would continue to abuse and assault children. The Roman Catholic sexual-abuse crisis is not simply a story of low-ranking priests with mental disorders who sexually assault people, including children; it is a story of priests, bishops, and popes who choose to idolize themselves and their power rather than protect the vulnerable people entrusted to them.

When seeking to understand the "how" of the sexual-abuse crisis, many scholars point to the cultural phenomenon of clericalism. In their study of the sexual-abuse crisis, theologians Julie Hanlon Rubio and Paul Schutz define clericalism as

> a structure of power that isolates clergy and sets priests above and apart, granting them excessive authority, trust, rights, and responsibilities while diminishing the agency of lay people and religious.[3]

Clericalism is a culture of abuse and, ultimately, a culture of death. Its unique structures create a caste system of superior men who enjoy an all-too-easily abused authority. The main goal of this chapter is to expand the preceding definition of clericalism. Our aim is not to provide an exhaustive account of clericalism and its history.[4] Rather, we focus our attention on

---

[3] Julie Hanlon Rubio and Paul Schutz, *Beyond 'Bad Apples': Understanding Clergy Perpetrated Sexual Abuse as a Structural Problem and Cultivating Strategies for Change* (Santa Clara, CA: 2022), 1.

[4] For examinations of clericalism in the Catholic Church, see George B. Wilson, *Clericalism: The Death of Priesthood* (Collegeville, MN: Liturgical

two aspects of clericalism that play a central role in perpetuating the sexual-abuse crisis.

Triumphalism: Clerics as Above and Apart

To begin our description of clericalist culture, we turn our attention to triumphalism. Simply defined, triumphalism is an "attitude or feeling of victory or superiority" that is held over others.[5] Those whose hubris leads them to see everyone else as incapable and inferior adversaries, they suffer from triumphalism. In a broader context, collective triumphalism among citizens of a country can be called nationalism. These people are not only convinced that their country is "the greatest country in the world," but they also feel that it is their country's right to behave as it sees fit regarding international relations. The sovereignty and dignity of other countries is not taken seriously, and their cultures are seen as underdeveloped and inferior. In a religious context, triumphalism is the mindset that one's religious tradition is radically unique and superior to all alternatives. Religious triumphalists see their own religion as infallible and the only tradition offering complete truth. These believers feel that they are the only truly moral community, the only shining beacon in a world of darkness, the lone ark in a vast flood. Due to this arrogance, religious triumphalists pejoratively label people of other religions as heathens, pagans, and infidels. Often, their most fervent ire is reserved for members of their own communities who they see as inadequate. These people are often labeled as sinners, heretics, and apostates. At best, they are viewed with paternalistic pity. At worst, they are

---

Press, 2008); Marie Keenan, *Child Sexual Abuse and the Catholic Church: Gender, Power, and Organizational Culture* (New York: Oxford University Press, 2013); James F. Keenan, "Hierarchicalism," *Theological Studies* 83, no. 1 (2022): 84–108.

[5] Merriam-Webster Dictionary, s.v. "triumphalism."

seen as a disease that threatens the health of the community. As such, religious triumphalism is a deeply naive and uncritical opinion of one's own religious tradition. It is tantamount to a fundamentalism that sees faith as a form of certainty with little to no room for doubt and questioning.

The Roman Catholic culture of clericalism adopts this triumphalist attitude and extends it even further to view ordained ministers (especially the pope and other bishops) as members of an elite brotherhood of consecrated men who rule the Church. In other words, clericalism places clerics both above and apart from the unordained and the unbaptized. Once ordained, these clerics are the guardians and gatekeepers of the sacred treasures (both spiritual and material) contained within the Roman Catholic Tradition. These men are often viewed as divine figures enjoying dictatorial authority over all facets of the Church's life. In an address delivered in 2018, Pope Francis described clericalism as arising "from an elitist and exclusivist vision of vocation, that interprets the ministry received as a power to be exercised rather than as a free and generous service to be given."[6] Within a triumphalist framework, power becomes a tool used for control. Once such triumphalist power becomes part of the equation, clericalist culture becomes an abusive cycle of elitism and exclusion.

Within this framework clergy often develop an identity rooted in an elevated sense of authority, viewing themselves as physical embodiments of God's presence. Triumphalist behaviors manifest in the conviction that the clergy possess exclusive access to divine truth, granting them authority over the subordinate, secular world. In Pope Francis's 2018 address, he says that clericalism leads clerics (and those who idolize

---

[6] Pope Francis, "Address by His Holiness Pope Francis at the Opening of the Synod of Bishops on Young People, the Faith and Vocational Discernment."

them) "to believe that we belong to a group that has all the answers and no longer needs to listen or learn anything." A clericalist culture has nothing to learn from those outside the brotherhood. The clergy, entrusted with the task of discerning and communicating God's will, often view themselves as the gatekeepers of spiritual wisdom and the salvation it offers.

Clericalism is essentially abusive. Yet, precisely because they have grown up in this culture, many Roman Catholics struggle to see clericalism as problematic. The term *abuse* is often reserved to describe only the most violent physical acts, when abusers seem to have lost control of themselves. However, this viewpoint fails to recognize the day-to-day culture of authoritarianism and control as forms of abuse. In reality, the horrifying acts of physical violence are not at all a loss of control; they are the logical result of a triumphalist culture that sees leaders (for example, parents, coaches, bishops, and so on) as people who are set above and apart from those they rule.[7] Indeed, clericalism is so hard to recognize as an abusive perversion of power because it often presents itself through language and practices that Roman Catholics have been formed to accept as holy and divinely revealed. For example, much of the traditional theological language used to describe ordained ministers may engage triumphalism, but it is difficult to critique because it has such a central place in biblical interpretation and doctrinal tradition. Consider these two brief examples.

One traditional phrase that is used to describe the role of ordained priests and bishops is the Latin phrase *in persona Christi capitis*, which is rendered in English as "in the

---

[7] This myth of losing control is explored in depth in Lundy Bancroft, *Why Does He Do That? Inside the Minds of Angry and Controlling Men* (New York: The Berkley Publishing Group, 2003); Jane Mockton Smith, *In Control: Dangerous Relationships and How They Lead to Murder* (London: Bloomsbury Circus, 2021).

person of Christ the head" (*LG*, #10).[8] This phrase is used to describe the role of the ordained minister when they are carrying out their vocation to serve the Church, especially when offering the Eucharistic sacrifice. In essence, this phrase is used to emphasize the Roman Catholic belief that Jesus is acting through the actions of the minister. When he speaks, Jesus is speaking. When he breaks the bread, Jesus breaks the bread. As we mentioned in the previous chapter, defining the minister's role this way runs a two-fold risk. First, by overemphasizing the minister's identity with Christ, it can eclipse other ways that Christ is truly present in the liturgy. Second, this language can over-emphasize the liturgy (and the minister in particular) as a source that *dispenses* grace. By describing ordained ministers as the only ones acting in the person of Christ, the clergy are distinguished from the laity (set apart) and elevated to a divine status (set above). Clearly, this language does not automatically cause an attitude of triumphalism. In fact, one could correctly argue that in a perfect world this traditional, doctrinal language would be used to instill humility in a minister, helping him and the rest of the Church focus on an encounter with Christ. Yet, it is evident that, when a man is formed to exclusively see himself as Christ, particularly in his role as authority figure, the opportunity for abuse is never far away.

The harmful risks of triumphalist language are exacerbated when coupled with our second example. Perhaps the most pervasive triumphalist language that is used for ordained ministers is that of "shepherd." Deeply biblical in its origins, this pastoral metaphor is intended to describe the protective and authoritative vocation of the minister. The English word

---

[8] *Catechism of the Catholic Church, Second Edition, Revised in Accordance with the Official Latin Text Promulgated by Pope John Paul II* (Vatican City: Libreria Editrice Vaticana, 1997), #1548.

pastor is even rooted in the Latin word for shepherd. A bishop serves as the primary pastor of his entire diocese, carrying a shepherd's staff known as a crozier as a symbol of his authority. In one of his most famous quotes, Pope Francis used this metaphor in order to exhort ordained ministers to *avoid* seeing themselves as above and apart from the laity. In a 2013 homily given during his first Chrism Mass as pope, Francis encouraged the priests in attendance to avoid separating themselves from those they serve. It was a warning *against* triumphalism: "This I ask you: be shepherds with, the 'odor of the sheep.'" Pope Francis wants Catholic ministers to lead lives *with* the people they serve. He wants pastors who know and love the members of their communities.

Much like the phrase *in persona Christi,* the metaphor of the shepherd *should* be used to help ministers see themselves as servants who are meant to lay down their lives for their sheep (Jn 10:11). Yet, as we have seen in recent decades (and not for the first time in the Church's history), there are pastors who are quite willing to lay down the lives of their sheep to protect their own power. Indeed, the psalmist attests to the dangers of pastoral metaphors in Psalm 44: "You have made us like sheep for slaughter" (Ps 44:11). In reality, shepherds are protecting a commodity. Like any good farmer, they might deeply care for the animals, but the animals are still helpless, unintelligent, and destined for slaughter. Clericalist triumphalism forms ordained ministers who see their communities primarily as sheep and treat their people as mere commodities, expendable and impersonal in the exercise of the priestly vocation.

Neither of these metaphors is intrinsically or exclusively harmful. By their nature, metaphors are ambiguous, deriving their meaning from context. Yet, using them uncritically is a profound mistake. In the recent history of the Church, systemic CPSA and the traumas that it has left in its wake form the context that gives these traditional metaphors their meaning. Insisting on repeating one's preferred biblical and doctrinal language regardless of the evident harms they are causing in the moment is yet another remarkable example of triumphalism that cares little for the most vulnerable. Insisting that the laity need more catechesis in order to better understand their own tradition is merely a deflection that chooses to see the "sheep's" confusion as the problem. Such insistence, especially if done solely for the sake of tradition, indicates a thriving culture of clericalism.

Through these triumphalist attitudes and the language that cultivates them, clericalism perpetuates systemic CPSA by insisting that clergy have been deserving of deference because they alone speak on behalf of God. Because they are fundamentally seen as sheep, the laity are expected to be docile, deferent, and silent. Because their role in the body of Christ is somewhere beneath the head, their dignity and value is derived from their subordination to their leaders. In other words, triumphalism creates a sense of divinely ordained entitlement. The clergy are entitled to followers who treat them like gods. Based on testimony from survivors of CPSA and their families, the perception of the clergy as representatives of God was often the reason that children were not believed and abusers were not confronted. It was seen as inappropriate and disrespectful to insinuate that a member of the clergy would be capable of such abuse. Further, when the abuse did become known, many bishops, including popes John Paul II and Benedict XVI, insisted that these matters be dealt with by the Church itself. Rather than referring to these abuses as crimes that should be dealt with by the authority of the state governments, bishops often described the crimes using the language of "sin" as a way of maintaining their moral authority.[9]

---

[9] Sophia Rita Jadda, "The Catholic Church Sex Abuse Crisis: The Rhetoric of Pope John Paul II, Benedict XVI and Francis," *Journal of Modern and Contemporary Christianity* 1, no. 1 (2022): 127–56.

Because the bishops and their clergy are seen as the primary presence of God's will and authority in this world, no other moral authority should have jurisdiction over the Church's "sins." In this way triumphalism creates a form of clericalism that allows systemic CPSA to go unchecked.

Interchangeability: Clerics with Excessive Rights and Responsibilities

In addition to triumphalism, another prevalent marker of Roman Catholic clericalist culture is the interchangeability of ordained ministers. Priests and bishops can be and are often moved from one parish or diocese to another without consultation with the communities they are serving. Because an ordained minister's primary role is to preside over liturgical celebrations, the most important part of their identity is the simple fact that they have been ordained, making them part of an elite caste who enjoy the exclusive right and responsibility to lead and control the liturgical life of the Church. Of course, there are many other pastoral and administrative duties the ordained ministers must carry out, but the rites of ordination attest to the fact that presiding over the liturgy is the primary vocation of the priest.

During an ordination liturgy, after the ordaining bishop lays hands on the man being ordained and says the prayer of ordination, the priest's hands are anointed with sacred chrism and he is given a chalice with wine and a paten holding bread. The bishops says, "Receive the oblation of the holy people to be offered to God."[10] The rites of ordination fundamentally serve to consecrate a priest into an order of men with the right and responsibility to celebrate the sacrifice of the mass on behalf of the people of God. His unique personality and

---

[10] The Roman Pontifical, Second Typical Edition, *Rite of Ordination of a Bishop, of Priests, and of Deacons*, #135.

his particular history that might radically distinguish him from other ordained priests have no bearing on his ability and duty to preside over the liturgy. When a Roman Catholic walks into a church to celebrate the liturgy, it is not supposed to matter how old the priest is, where he grew up, or what cultures he might come from. As long as he was validly ordained, he can validly celebrate the liturgy, and thereby exercise the power of his vocation: sanctifying the people of God by offering sacrifices on their behalf.

The hierarchical nature of clericalism results in a caste of spiritual leaders who exclusively enjoy the power of dispensing the grace necessary for salvation. The result, to use the language of Rubio and Schutz, is a group of men whose excessive rights and responsibilities eclipse the role of the laity in God's plan of salvation.[11] The laity are relegated to the passive role of lining up to accept the grace that these interchangeable clerics dispense. This way of describing the vocation of the priesthood is deeply clericalist because it ignores the fact that each unique ordained minister is meant to be a pastor *of a particular community*.

While we will return to this issue in greater detail, we can briefly say that, since the earliest centuries of Christianity, pastors were not defined by their membership in an elite class but by their pastoral role within a community of Christians. As theologian Richard Gaillardetz has pointed out, in the early decades of Christianity, pastors were asked to preside over the liturgy because they had shown themselves to be good and thoughtful pastors with unique gifts that fit with the unique needs of the community that they were serving.[12] They were not assumed to be pastoral leaders because they had the power

---

[11] Rubio and Schutz, *Beyond 'Bad Apples,'* 1.

[12] Richard Gaillardetz, "A Church in Crisis: How Did We Get Here? How Do We Move Forward?" *Worship* 70, no. 4 (December 2018): 209–10.

and authority to dispense grace through the liturgy. It is often assumed that someone should lead a community because they have been ordained. In reality, they should be ordained because they have shown themselves to be a capable and trustworthy leader of the community. Put simply, Christian pastors were defined by their relationship to the people they served, not by a special liturgical power they possessed. The idea that one pastor could be relocated and assigned to a community that was foreign to him would have made little sense to early Christians, especially if that community had not provided its input on the matter. In fact, in the early centuries of Christianity bishops were normally elected by the people they would lead.[13] Input from the laity was an essential step in determining if a bishop did indeed have a vocation to lead a particular community. Obviously, this meant that the laity enjoyed a great deal of influence in choosing the clerics who guided their communities. By insisting that ordained ministers are interchangeable whenever a bishop sees fit, clericalism today allows clergy to maintain power over the laity and particular clergy to maintain power over other clergy. Clericalism denies that a pastor is defined by his relationship to the unique community of people he is called to serve; rather, a minister is defined by his consecration into a sacred caste of powerful men. As we stated in the previous chapter, an ordained minister is meant to be a symbol that embodies the love of Christ, providing the laity with a personal encounter with the grace of God's divine love. They are meant to be symbols that provocatively offer the grace of God. Instead, clericalism reduces ordained ministers to impersonal technicians who are functionally all the same.

Culturally, clericalism maintains power by insisting that ordained ministers are interchangeable and can be relocated to a new community when the relevant bishops see fit. As has been

---

[13] Gaillardetz, 218–19.

meticulously documented, over the past fifty years the practice of transferring abusive ordained ministers (both priests and bishops) from one parish or diocese to another was one of the ways that bishops were so readily able to cover up egregious cases of abuse. In order for the Church to maintain its power and manage its public perception, bishops would move an abusive priest to a parish where the community was unaware of his crimes.[14] Later, the Church would defend this action as misguided, eventually going so far as to blame psychologists who claimed to approve of this practice. However, when following the trail of internal memos between Church officials, alongside reports from canon lawyers such as Thomas Doyle, who vehemently opposed the practice, it is clear that evidence of the failed attempts existed.[15] Although internal critics spoke out against the practice, and patterns of abuse continued, the Church did not change its practice and continued to move priests between parishes, successfully protecting them from local authorities and confrontation from those who had experienced abuse.

In her book *Truth and Repair: How Trauma Survivors Envision Justice*, Dr. Judith L. Herman tells the story of a man named "Daniel" who was a survivor of CPSA. Daniel had been sexually abused by Fr. Paul Shanley, a Catholic priest in the Archdiocese of Boston. Despite being aware of Shanley's history of sexually abusing children, the archdiocese relocated him to a parish in California. In recounting his experience to Herman, Daniel said the following:

> [Shanley's] sick and he's dangerous . . . and they knew that, and they didn't do anything about it. They kept

---

[14] For substantial evidence of this practice, see BishopAccountability.org, "Assignment Record Project."

[15] Onell R. Soto, "Church, Lawyers Latch on to Federal Case," *Union-Tribune*, August 29, 2005.

assigning him to places where he would be with kids, and they kept not notifying people.... They should have known better.[16]

While the case of Fr. Shanley is particularly egregious, it is by no means the only example of a clericalist culture that sought to protect itself and its power by interchanging clerics despite knowing the horrifying risks.[17] Whether consciously or subconsciously motivated by clericalism, bishops have considered it their right and responsibility to relocate these abusive priests. One result of these fraudulent decisions has been an increase in the numbers of abuse, leaving people and their communities deeply traumatized. The scandal of betrayal has been another result of this behavior.

Because ordained ministers are interchangeable members of an elite caste, the moral failures of some bishops and priests have a wide-ranging impact on the reputation of all the caste's members. Many priests who have never personally abused a person or perpetrated a cover-up are horrified by the crimes of their fellow clerics. Yet, because clericalism has spent centuries overemphasizing their shared elite status, every member of the clergy now carries the connotations of abuse and abuser. Precisely because it insists on their interchangeability, clericalist culture implicates all clerics in the scandal of systemic CPSA. Yes, the sexual abuse of minors is undeniably an egregious crime, but it is by no means the only abuse being perpetrated by the culture of clericalism. Clericalism systemically denigrates the laity and strips them of their dignity and authority as baptized members of the body of Christ. Clericalism also denigrates presbyters by erasing

---

[16] Judith L. Herman, *Truth and Repair: How Trauma Survivors Envision Justice* (London: Basic Books, 2023), 134.

[17] BishopAccountability.org, "Assignment Record Project."

their unique gifts and personalities, forcing them, instead, to be homogenous pawns in the strategies of bishops and other hierarchs. They are effectively cut off from the particular communities they love and are taught to see their self-erasure as some heroic virtue. Triumphalism and the interchangeability of clerics collaborate to cultivate a context wherein the clergy are able to assume excessive authority and control over the life of the Church. The clergy, especially the bishops, demand an incredible level of trust while refusing accountability to those they serve. As ethicist James Keenan has rightly noted, the bishops of the Roman Catholic Church have curated a culture of impunity that they wear like righteous armor.[18] One need only examine the legal responses of the bishops to see the ways that clericalism still motivates their response to the abuse they have inflicted.

Impunity:
Clerics Demanding Excessive Trust and Authority

Italian author Umberto Eco's novel *The Name of the Rose* tells a story of a murder investigation undertaken at a Benedictine abbey. One of the monks has mysteriously died, and the abbot accepts help from a Franciscan friar to determine the cause of death. As the abbot is explaining the task to the investigator, he asks for the friar's discretion:

> In this abbey something has happened that requires the attention and counsel of an acute and prudent man such as you are. Acute in uncovering, and prudent (if necessary) in covering. If a shepherd errs, he must be isolated

---

[18] James F. Keenan, "Hierarchicalism."

from other shepherds, but woe unto us if the sheep begin to distrust shepherds.[19]

The last line tells the reader that the abbot is deeply concerned about the way one monk's sins could damage the reputation and authority of the entire clergy. The sheep only need to know as much as is necessary to keep them trustful and obedient. This short vignette is an excellent literary example of the abusive attitudes that arise out of clericalism. The abbot feels no sense of accountability to his sheep precisely because he sees them as sheep. In his clericalist mind the greater good is to protect the holy reputation of the clergy. So, he orders a cover-up.

As we saw in our previous two sections, triumphalism and an interchangeable clergy are just two aspects of a clericalist culture that prioritizes its own power over all else. In this final section we recount some of the legal and financial strategies the Church has used to assert and maintain its authority. Operating as one of the wealthiest and most notoriously insular global institutions, the exact nature of Church assets and financial strategy remains, to some extent, a mystery. However, evidence has revealed the strategic use of large financial settlements to silence individuals who experienced clergy sex abuse.[20] Such revelations unveil a Church that avoids confrontation with victims and, to an even greater degree, seeks to prevent the potential for public scandal at any financial cost.

As the crisis of systemic CPSA mounted and victims began threatening to bring the cases to the courts, news of the crisis

---

[19] Umberto Eco, *The Name of the Rose* (New York: Harcourt, Brace and Company, 1980).

[20] Thomas G. Plante and Kathleen L. McChesney, *Sexual Abuse in the Catholic Church: A Decade in Crisis, 2002–2012* (Westport, CT: Praeger Publishers, 2011), 135.

reached beyond the individual dioceses in question. Thomas Doyle, a Catholic priest and canon lawyer serving the Vatican, was among the first to bring internal attention to the scale of the crisis and the potential for financial and legal ruin if the Church neglected to make significant changes to the policy. After reviewing the 1980 South Louisiana case of Gilbert Gauthe, in which Gauthe abused over one hundred children across multiple dioceses, Doyle wrote an internal, confidential report warning of the mounting financial, legal, and ethical troubles ahead if the handling of abuse allegations did not change, particularly if the common and markedly ineffective practice of moving priests continued.[21] Doyle's report would be ignored by his superiors, and he was warned by his direct supervisor that continuing to focus on such cases of abuse would end his career as a canon lawyer.[22] In later interviews Doyle recalls his self-described naivete in assuming the Church would respond to the report and the complete erosion of his trust in the institutional Church, illustrated in his choice to leave the priesthood and dedicate the rest of his career to working with survivors and critiquing the Catholic Church as an institution.[23]

Doyle's experience with the internal resistance to critique of and reform for the Church's policy surrounding the handling of abuse allegations reflects the damage that internal secrecy and resistance to critique can inflict on clergy who do attempt to bring change and attention to pressing matters. Because he was a member of the elite, ordained "brotherhood," he was supposed to protect his fellow clerics above all else. Clericalism

---

[21] Thomas Doyle, *The Problem of Sexual Molestation by Roman Catholic Clergy: Meeting the Problem in a Comprehensive and Responsible Manner* (June 1985).

[22] Jeremy Rogalski and Tina Macias, "Catholic Priest Shuns Collar to Fight for Survivors of Clergy Sexual Abuse" (May 10, 2019).

[23] Rogalski and Macias.

created a situation in which, during a time of crisis and abuse, internal calls to action were actively silenced. Due to the effects that clericalism had on internal cleric relations, whistleblowers such as Doyle were forced to choose between a level of loyalty that sacrificed the safety of the community or dismissal from the Church to which they had dedicated their lives.

Beyond the devastating internal response, when individuals who experienced CPSA sought legal refuge and recourse, the Church's response again sought to minimize abuse and quickly quell the accusations through financial payouts. Contrary to later claims by Church officials that called those who had experienced CPSA and were seeking restitution "litigation-happy" and financially motivated, financial settlements were often the last resort for individuals who were directly affected and their families.[24] In the words of survivor of CPSA, Dan Ronan, "You know, a check doesn't change anything. It doesn't make me whole. It doesn't turn back the clock fifty-some-odd years. It doesn't do any of that. It just gives you some compensation."[25] Psychologist Mary Frawley-O'Dea describes the experience survivors had when seeking accountability from the Catholic Church:

> At the core of the survivor's being, the worst has happened yet again; he has been paid off to go away while life goes on relatively untouched for the perpetrator and those who shielded him. . . . Many survivors, in fact, resorted to lawsuits only after being stonewalled in their quest for more personal reparative gestures.[26]

---

[24] Plante and McChesney, *Sexual Abuse in the Catholic Church*, 111.

[25] In Scott Simon, "A Survivor of Abuse by a Catholic Priest in Chicago Shares His Experience," NPR.org, May 27, 2023.

[26] Mary Gail Frawley-O'Dea, "The Experience of the Victim of Sexual Abuse: a Reflection," United States Conference of Catholic Bishops (June 13, 2002).

The experience Frawley-O'Dea describes is not unique. Throughout the history of systemic CPSA, the Catholic Church's responses to accusations of abuse exhibit a pattern of gross negligence and intentional avoidance. When thinking of the sheer amount of money paid by the Catholic Church in settlements, it may seem as though it has provided care for the laity. However, further reflection and investigation into the lived experience of survivors reveals that financial incentives were a last resort that was meant to curtail the potential for individuals who experienced CPSA to be heard by the courts, government authorities, and—perhaps most crucially—the general public.[27]

While the amount of money paid out by the Catholic Church in response to CPSA lawsuits reaches into the billions of dollars, more than substantiating Doyle's warning, the financial aspect of the CPSA scandal serves only as a means to highlight the incredibly devastating consequences that occur when a culture of clericalism is perpetuated. An organizational culture that demands secrecy, refuses accountability, and actively attempts to silence whistleblowers results in damage that cannot be undone by financial settlements.[28] Instead of relying on money to solve all problems, the focus must be on dismantling the culture of clericalism that perpetuated such abuse and used financial settlements in an attempt to sustain a dangerous, abusive clerical culture in the first place.

Combining triumphalism with fears of negative publicity, the American Catholic Church sought to settle cases before individuals who experienced CPSA could seek intervention

---

[27] Sarah Fowler, "'A Nightmare,' Man Tells All, Says He Was Abused by Mississippi Priest More than 75 Times," *The Clarion-Ledger* online, January 23, 2019.

[28] Simon, "A Survivor of Abuse by a Catholic Priest in Chicago Shares His Experience."

from government authorities.²⁹ As may be expected, such reporting would place the Church in a precarious legal position. However, beyond the legal nightmare, answering to a government authority threatened the culture of clericalism. Such legal repercussions had the potential to force the Church to concede its image as the ultimate moral authority, damaging the triumphalist perception of clerics as the voice of God.

As we mentioned above, many bishops described the cases of sexual abuse as sinful acts and not as crimes.³⁰ Such frameworks reinforced the Church's resistance to secular oversight, refusing to accept accountability to institutions that they viewed as beneath them. As they fought to maintain the boundary between the Catholic Church and governmental authorities, the Church often appealed to the American constitutional right that mandates freedom of religion. Citing canonical laws, which require absolute allegiance and an emphasis on avoiding scandal, the hierarchy resisted civil laws that would label ordained ministers as mandatory reporters, requiring them to report abuse to civil authorities.³¹ Their resistance ultimately sought to protect the image of clergy as divine figures beyond the reach of earthly judgment.

As the 1980s and 1990s brought growing questions surrounding the Church as an institution and its negligence in protecting children, canon lawyers for the Catholic Church began to argue that they had made attempts to rehabilitate priests with therapy and, therefore, could not be held criminally negligent. In their arguments Church attorneys cited a lack of knowledge that the rehabilitation process would not work. With this strategy the Church sought to portray the

---

[29] Fowler, "'A Nightmare.'"

[30] Wilson, *Clericalism*, 73.

[31] Christopher R. Pudelski, "The Constitutional Fate of Mandatory Reporting Statutes and the Clergy-Communicant Privilege in a Post-Smith World," *Northwestern University Law Review* 98, no. 2 (2002): 703–38.

serial abusers as unusual circumstances and unique cases in which the predetermined pathway to recovery just happened not to work. However, later investigations, such as that from the attorney general of Massachusetts in 2003, uncovered internal Church records that revealed an institution that had been made aware of its failings but refused adequately to inform other dioceses and refused to supervise priests who were deemed needing supervision to be safely reintegrated into Church settings.[32]

Ironically, one of the revealing pieces of evidence proving the Church's concerted effort to hide the sex-abuse crisis was a disturbing lack of evidence. The discovery that Boston court proceedings regarding cases of childhood sex abuse in the Church were sealed, with only "skeletal remains" left, was central to the *Boston Globe*'s reporting, spurring on continued investigations from journalists.[33] As groups of survivors began to organize and speak to the media, calls for public access to court documents regarding the sex-abuse crisis exploded.

As is retold in the 2015 movie *Spotlight*, the investigation from the *Boston Globe* uncovered more than a pattern of predatory priests. Instead, as they dug into court records, a story of "a bunch of lawyers turning child abuse into a cottage industry" emerged.[34] The legal aspect of the Church cover-up cannot be overstated. Beyond flexing their financial power through settlements, the individuals who sought legal recourse

---

[32] Thomas F. Reilly, *The Sexual Abuse of Children in the Roman Catholic Archdiocese of Boston*, Office of the Attorney General Commonwealth of Massachusetts (July 23, 2003), 25–68.

[33] Matt Carroll, Sacha Pfeiffer, and Michael Rezendes, "Church Allowed Abuse by Priest for Years," *The Boston Globe: The Globe Spotlight*, January 6, 2002.

[34] *Spotlight*, directed by Tom McCarthy, Entertainment 1, September 3, 2015.

witnessed the level of aggression with which the Church would try to protect its own, with Church lawyers attempting to expunge direct references to abusive clergy and, when asked to recall individual abuse cases in a grand jury, showing a troubling inability to recall cases over which they had presided.[35]

The successful sealing of legal filings and the attempts on behalf of the Church to maintain their confidentiality as the public began demanding answers only further eroded the trust of the laity in the Catholic institution. The Church was clearly aware of the crisis and yet intentionally hid the truth from the laity in order to protect its self-appointed moral high ground. The culture of clericalism lies beneath these audacious legal and financial attempts at a cover-up. While the rate of abuse from priests may not be disproportionate from that of the wider population, the true crisis lies in the culture of clericalism.[36] Clericalism is a culture of death and a toxic root, creating an environment where abuse flourishes in the shadows, protected by a demand for secrecy.

In short, the bishops and the other clergy they control operated with impunity, refusing accountability until it was unavoidable. Rampant triumphalism imbued them with a sense of entitlement that allowed them to demand vicious amounts of trust from their fellow clergy and the laity. Clericalism forms clergy to treat the laity like the commodity sheep, there only for slaughter. Any of these sheep who vocally criticize the clergy fail to be the pious Catholics to which clericalism feels entitled. Those who demand accountability are failing to be the docile and deferent sheep that the clergy deserve.

---

[35] Roseanne Bonventre, "Suffolk Supreme Court Special Grand Jury Report," May 6, 2002.

[36] John Jay College of Criminal Justice, "The Nature and Scope of Sexual Abuse of Minors by Catholic Priests and Deacons in the United States 1950–2002," United States Conference of Catholic Bishops (February 2004).

Conclusion:
Clericalism Facilitating Trauma

In his 2018 "Letter to the People of God" Pope Francis forcefully describes the link between the CPSA crisis and the clericalist culture that continues to make it possible: "We have realized that these wounds never disappear and that they require us forcefully to condemn these atrocities and join forces in uprooting this culture of death." The horrifying accounts of sexual abuse are indeed atrocities that need to be condemned, and virtually every member of the Church, from the laity to the bishops, has done so. However, the scandal of systemic CPSA is far more than individual acts of sexual assault. To use a common metaphor, CPSA is a symptom of clericalism's disease. If the Church is going to address this crisis adequately, then it cannot be content to only create policy safeguards that protect children from potential abusers.

For example, in the United States the *Dallas Charter* is one example of a laudable undertaking in which clergy are collaborating with laity to develop procedures for addressing allegations of sexual abuse, as well as develop "guidelines for reconciliation, healing, accountability, and prevention of future acts of abuse."[37] While the *Dallas Charter* has done much to encourage priests' accountability to civil authorities, ensuring that vulnerable children are better protected, it has done far too little to address directly the culture of clericalism that undergirds the crisis. Even when the *Dallas Charter* requires review boards to be composed of lay members of the Church, those boards are limited to an advisory role that only makes recommendations. Those recommendations can

---

[37] United States Conference of Catholic Bishops, "Promise to Protect: Pledge to Heal (Washington, DC: USCCB, 2018 <2002>). Commonly referred to as the *Dallas Charter*.

easily be refused by the committee of bishops that reserves all executive power.[38]

The triumphalism that sets clerics above and apart still flourishes in Roman Catholicism. The Church must continue to do the good work of protecting its people and reducing the numbers of sexual-abuse cases. However, that work cannot be allowed to replace or distract from the cultural reform necessary at every level of the Church.

In our previous chapter we argued that clericalism prefers a liturgy where the laity are passive and silent. The result is a liturgy that often fails to realize its goal: a Church that becomes more alive with the love of Christ. In this chapter we have argued that clericalism is willing to extort silence (or, if necessary, buy it), because silence is what clericalism already expects from the laity. The sexual-abuse crisis is not simply the story of "a few bad apples" who have failed to live up to their vocation. The sexual-abuse crisis is a story of a culture of death that, due to the courageous witness and tireless work of survivors and their allies, continues to reap the consequences of its crimes. Because it is a centuries-old culture that spans the globe, clericalism is not going to be quickly or easily changed. Well-meaning bishops and priests are still defending exclusivist and elitist theologies of ordained ministry despite being shown repeatedly the horrors that result from such perversions of power. If clericalism is allowed to endure under

---

[38] For example, in the "2022 Annual Report: Findings and Recommendations" published by the Secretariat of Child and Youth Protection, Suzanne Healy (chair of the National Review Board) recounted that the board of lay advisers "had previously recommended a singular day in which every parish in every diocese and eparchy would offer a liturgy of lament for victim survivors of clergy abuse and their families." This recommendation was refused. Yet, as a testament to the good will of many Catholic leaders (both clergy and lay) many parishes chose to hold liturgies and other events to express solidarity with those who have been affected by systemic CPSA.

the guise of a "traditional ministerial priesthood," then the instances of abuse that seem to have subsided in recent years will inevitably return.

To conclude, not all ordained ministers in the Roman Catholic Church are intentional advocates of clericalism. In fact, one would be hard-pressed to find a single cleric who would proudly identify as such. Much like racism or sexism, clericalism is a culture that operates clandestinely and often at a subconscious level. Clericalism results in leaders with good intentions who remain complicit in perpetuating abusive structures. There are many ordained ministers who struggle mightily against clericalist culture and the traumas it has inflicted. There are many deacons, priests, and bishops who are dedicated to ending the abuses of clericalism. Yet, as Gerald Arbuckle has pointed out, cultures are exceedingly difficult to change.[39] Eradicating a culture, especially one that centralizes power as viciously as clericalism does, requires inflicting deep personal loss on those who have lived in the culture for their entire lives. The rest of this book attempts to imagine how such cultural changes might unfold.

How do abuse and trauma affect those who endure it? How do they affect those who inflict it? How do those effects influence the liturgical life of the Church? If the liturgy is meant to be the source and summit of grace, how can it realize its purpose amid a culture of death?

---

[39] Gerald A. Arbuckle, *Abuse and Cover-up: Refounding the Catholic Church in Trauma* (Maryknoll, NY: Orbis Books, 2019).

3

The Real Presence of Violence

PTSD and the Liturgy

> *A young woman who was a [former] altar server told me that the chaplain, her superior as an altar server, always introduced the sexual abuse he was committing against her with the words: "This is my body which will be given up for you." It is obvious that this woman can no longer hear the very words of consecration without experiencing again all the horrific distress of her abuse.*
> —Pope Benedict XVI

In the first chapter we argued that the liturgy is a ritual process meant to cultivate grace in the life of the Church. In order for this goal to be realized, those who participate in the liturgy must have the proper dispositions that allow them to experience the liturgy as a provocative invitation into God's friendship. As we described in the previous chapter, the Roman Catholic Church's clericalist culture has inflicted vast amounts of pain and suffering on many members of the Church, and those traumas have done immense damage to the liturgical life of the Church. In order to work against this culture of death, as it has been called by Pope Francis, and work toward healing the Church, we must first understand the extent of this trauma's impact on the liturgy. To that end, this and the following two chapters examine some of the ways that the traumas inflicted by systemic clergy perpetrated sexual abuse (CPSA) have influenced the dispositions of Catholic worshipers and, therefore, the fruitfulness of the liturgical life of the Church. This chapter begins by describing trauma and post-traumatic stress disorder (PTSD). We then describe how PTSD can transform the liturgy into the real presence of violence. In these circumstances the liturgy doesn't merely fail to accomplish its purpose of being a source and summit of grace; it instead becomes a source and instrument of ongoing trauma and death.

What Is Trauma?

First, a caveat: definitions of trauma can be dangerous. The search for a cohesive and universal definition has been an ongoing challenge for those who study trauma. Many scholars recognize that trauma's effects are not easily categorized, because each person's unique history shapes how they experience an event and how that event affects them. For example, a car accident will likely be experienced differently by someone who just learned to drive than by someone who has been racing cars their entire life. Similarly, hearing nearby gunshots will be experienced differently by someone with a long history of hunting and firearm safety classes than by someone who has never held or heard a gun fired. All of these people might experience these events as traumatic, but *how* they experience the event can vary greatly due to their unique dispositions. Hence, any overly narrow definition of trauma runs the risk of excluding (and thereby overlooking) experiences that might help us better understand trauma.

Additionally, overly narrow definitions of trauma can result in people failing to receive the acknowledgment and care that they deserve.[1] This risk of failure to care makes definitions of trauma potentially dangerous. For example, in an article that examines the many ways that trauma has been defined and the diverse ways that people respond to traumatic events, psychologists George Bonanno and Anthony Mancini highlight historical controversy regarding definitions of trauma, especially its association with war-related dysfunction.[2] They point out that definitions of trauma are often controversial because when people are described as being traumatized, they are usually seen as deserving special attention and care. For example, in the context of military service, leaders who are concerned about soldiers using trauma as an excuse to avoid work might prefer a narrower definition of trauma that makes it more difficult for people to be relieved of their duties and afforded special care. However, as understandings of and research into the nature of trauma have evolved, it has become apparent that trauma can arise from any number of threatening events that might occur in a person's life.

In addition to the preference for strict and narrow definitions, it has become common in recent years to critique the perceived overuse of the term *trauma*. Some psychologists, such as the director of the Center for Clinical Psychology in Australia, Jon Finch, have voiced concern that uninformed and imprecise uses of the term *trauma*, often referred to as "concept creep," "dilutes its significance and may lead to confusion."[3]

---

[1] Bessel van der Kolk, *The Body Keeps the Score: Brain, Mind, and Body in the Healing of Trauma* (New York: Penguin Books, 2015), 166–68.

[2] George A. Bonanno and Anthony D. Mancini, "Beyond Resilience and PTSD: Mapping the Heterogeneity of Responses to Potential Trauma," *Psychological Trauma* 4, no. 1 (2012): 74–83.

[3] Jon Finch, "The Problem with Pop Psychology," The Centre for Clinical Psychology, November 14, 2023.

Policing the use of the term can prevent its misuse. For example, theologian Jennifer Beste has argued that, due to concept creep, definitions of trauma that are too broad can unintentionally disrespect the survivors of horrific violence, "because it minimizes and trivializes the extreme suffering of traumas like genocide, imminent threat to one's life, and sexual violence."[4] Bearing these concerns in mind, it is important to seek a balance between linguistic precision, on one hand, and compassion for those suffering the consequences of trauma, on the other. Recognizing that trauma exists on a spectrum and commonly defies the ease of categorization helps us remember that diagnostic concepts such as *trauma* and *PTSD* are a linguistic and diagnostic means to serve the health and well-being of people and society.

Much like the terms *abuse* and *violence,* the term *trauma* does not need to be reserved only for the most egregious instances of oppression and suffering. In fact, if we refuse to recognize and name more subtle forms of abuse and violence as such, then we can easily end up overlooking and maintaining the problematic cultures and events that cause more acute and egregious instances of abuse, violence, and trauma. As experts who work to address domestic violence will attest, being physically assaulted is abusive and traumatic, but so are the persistent emotional, financial, and spiritual abuses that perpetrators will use to control their victims.[5] By simply noting the complex nature of trauma and the imprecision that necessarily accompanies all attempts to describe its diverse consequences, we can cultivate a more inclusive and empathetic approach that

---

[4] Jennifer Beste, "Critical Reflections on the Discourse on a 'Traumatized Church,'" in *Theology in a Post-Traumatic Church*, ed. John N. Sheveland (Maryknoll, NY: Orbis Books, 2023), 52.

[5] For a closer examination of the different forms of abuse that can be part of an abusive culture, see Domestic Abuse Intervention Programs, "Understanding the Power and Control Wheel."

honors the diverse experiences of those who have undergone trauma. Hence, it is important to work continually toward a broad description of trauma that is always evolving in light of new insights and new testimonies. What follows, then, is not intended to be a fixed or exhaustive definition of trauma. Rather, we intend to offer one description of trauma that will help us better examine the Roman Catholic sex-abuse crisis, its diverse manifestations, and its ranging effects.

At its root, the English word *trauma* comes from the Greek word for "wound." In its original meaning the word indicated a physical wound created by an external force. However, as theologian Serene Jones points out, the term has come to be used more broadly to include other types of spiritual, emotional, and social consequences.[6] For instance, the Substance Abuse and Mental Health Services Administration (SAMHSA) defines *trauma* broadly as "an event, series of events, or set of circumstances that is experienced by an individual as physically or emotionally harmful or life threatening and that has lasting adverse effects on the individual's functioning and mental, physical, social, emotional, or spiritual well-being."[7] This definition may prompt one to interject that this is so broad that it would seem to imply that nearly all people have already or will at some point experience trauma. This insight is correct. Trauma and its effects are exceedingly common, yet they consistently go unrecognized, underappreciated, or flatly denied.

Because we are focusing our attention primarily on the Roman Catholic sexual-abuse crisis, whenever we use the term *trauma,* we are referring to a state of profound physical, psychological, and/or spiritual distress, sometimes experienced as feelings of terror, loss of control, and helplessness in the face

---

[6] Serene Jones, *Trauma and Grace: Theology in a Ruptured World* (Louisville, KY: Westminster John Knox Press, 2009), 12.

[7] SAMHSA, "What Is Trauma?" November 8, 2024.

of compounding stressors. It is important to note that trauma is not a type of event that can be easily distinguished from non-traumatic events. A car accident, a cancer diagnosis, the sudden death of a family member, experiencing an earthquake, and, central to this chapter, the witnessing or experiencing of CPSA are all potentially traumatic events. Here we follow Bonanno and Mancini in using the term *potentially traumatic events* because not all people experience events in the same way.[8] While an assault might cause someone pain, it will not necessarily be experienced as traumatic. Everyone experiences potentially traumatic events differently, and their reactions to these events dynamically unfold in the days, weeks, months, and years following the event. Hence, we describe trauma as a *state* of profound distress that can manifest itself in a wide variety of harmful responses. In other words, we cannot label an event as traumatic without thoughtfully and carefully seeking to understand how that event has affected the people who experienced or witnessed it.

Traumatic experiences are commonly described as having the power to shatter fundamental assumptions about one's self and the world in which we live. Trauma is not defined by specific types of events but by the subjective experiences and responses of individuals. Trauma, therefore, transcends mere events; it seeps deep into the very fabric of one's being, reshaping perceptions and fundamentally altering one's capacity to function. To use the words of psychologist and trauma researcher Bessel van der Kolk, "Trauma results in a fundamental reorganization of the way mind and brain manage perceptions. It changes not only how we think and what we think about, but also our very capacity to function."[9] The effects of trauma

---

[8] Bonanno and Mancini, "Beyond Resilience and PTSD," 76.
[9] Van der Kolk, *The Body Keeps the Score*, 34.

reverberate within the individual, taking shape in ways that resist easy categorization. From survivors of sexual abuse to witnesses of natural disasters, trauma leaves an indelible mark on an individuals, damaging their self-perception and their relationships with others.

As we will see through this and the following chapters, trauma has many consequences on those who experience it. For the rest of this chapter we focus on one significant consequence of trauma: post-traumatic stress disorder. In the next two chapters we examine moral injury and moral distress. These two conditions are often the results of experiencing a potentially traumatic event. We examine each of these conditions in order to emphasize the fact that people experience and respond to trauma differently. The term *traumatized,* therefore, should not be assumed to refer exclusively to people experiencing PTSD. Further, our focus on PTSD, moral injury, and moral distress is not intended to imply that these are the only or the most significant effects of trauma. Rather, we focus on these three conditions because they readily appear when one examines the effects that systemic CPSA has had on the liturgical life of the Church.

Post-Traumatic Stress Disorder

Now that we have described trauma generally, we move to examine one damaging consequence of trauma: post-traumatic stress disorder. Particularly important for this section, PTSD resulting from CPSA is a condition that can corrupt the worshiper's disposition that is necessary for the liturgy to serve fruitfully as a source and summit of grace. In such cases the liturgy fails to effectively offer God's love, instead causing the worshiper to reexperience the violence previously inflicted by the Church's clericalist culture.

Perhaps the most commonly used description of PTSD comes from the American Psychiatric Association's criteria in the *Diagnostic and Statistical Manual of Mental Disorders* (*DSM*). The *DSM* is revised every five to seven years to respond to psychiatric literature and stay up to date on the current understanding of psychiatric conditions. While the *DSM*'s diagnosing criteria can easily lead to an over-medicalization of a patient's experience and be too narrow at times, it nevertheless serves as a helpful starting point for understanding conditions. Rather than examining all aspects of the *DSM*'s description of PTSD, we focus our attention on those aspects of PTSD that relate to our consideration of how PTSD influences a worshiper's experience of the liturgy.

The most recent version of the *DSM*, the fifth edition with text revisions (*DSM-5–TR*), diagnoses PTSD when a person has

> exposure to actual or threatened death, serious injury, or sexual violence in one (or more) of the following ways: 1) Directly experiencing the traumatic event(s). 2) Witnessing, in person, the event(s) as it occurred to others. 3) Learning that the traumatic event(s) occurred to a close family member or close friend. In cases of actual or threatened death of a family member or friend, the event(s) must have been violent or accidental. 4) Experiencing repeated or extreme exposure to aversive details of the traumatic event(s) (e.g., first responders collecting human remains; police officers repeatedly exposed to details of child abuse).[10]

---

[10] Michael B. First, ed., *Diagnostic and Statistical Manual of Mental Disorders: DSM-5–TR*, fifth edition, text revision (American Psychiatric Association Publishing, 2022), 302–4.

Following the potentially traumatic event, the person must experience a variable combination of unpleasant symptoms like nightmares, distress when exposed to traumatic reminders, hypervigilance, or avoidance of feelings associated with the trauma. The symptoms must be disruptive to a person's life, and last at least a month.[11] This set of diagnostic criteria for PTSD provides clinicians with a general sense of the disorder and is most helpful in clinical settings. However, as is the case with definitions of trauma, the *DSM* has been criticized for its overly-narrow understanding of PTSD, which often comes at the expense of women.[12] Generally speaking, PTSD is understood as

> a mental health condition that's caused by an extremely stressful or terrifying event—either being part of it or witnessing it. Symptoms may include flashbacks, nightmares, severe anxiety and uncontrollable thoughts about the event.[13]

For the purposes of this chapter, we focus on one category of PTSD symptoms that can heavily influence the experience of liturgical worship: reexperiencing symptoms.

When listing the criteria necessary to diagnose PTSD, the *DSM-5-TR* lists five types of "intrusion symptoms" that a person might face: (1) intrusive and involuntary memories related to the traumatic event, (2) recurrent, distressing dreams related to the traumatic event, (3) dissociative flashbacks wherein one acts/feels as though the event were recurring, (4) psychological distress when exposed to reminders of the traumatic event,

---

[11] *DSM-5-TR*, 302–4.

[12] Lizette Gründlingh, "A Critique of the PTSD Definition of Trauma from a Woman's Perspective," University of Johannesburg, MA dissertation, 2010.

[13] Mayo Clinic, "Post-Traumatic Stress Disorder (PTSD)" (2024).

and (5) physiological reactivity when exposed to reminders of the traumatic event.[14] Understanding these reexperiencing symptoms is important because it allows us to better appreciate what is happening when liturgical symbols (for example, bread, vestments, kneeling, and so on) serve as triggers for symptoms of PTSD.

According to van der Kolk, "Dissociation is the essence of trauma.... The sensory fragments of memory intrude into the present where they are literally relived."[15] Experiencing a dissociative flashback means reliving a traumatic event where one feels as if they are in the traumatic event for the first time. These flashbacks are described as dissociative because the experience is severed from their current reality (that is, dissociated) and they are reimmersed in the traumatic event. This is an involuntary and visceral reliving, where the emotions and felt reactions to a trigger are indistinguishable from the experience of the initial trauma itself. This is an emotional and physiological experience that happens regardless of whether the person experiencing it is safe or not. That is, an innocent or well-meaning action may provoke a flashback, forcing someone to relive something horrifying or painful. For many military veterans, holidays that involve the widespread use of fireworks are horrifying events because the sounds and feelings of exploding fireworks can trigger flashbacks of combat, causing them to relive terrifying moments of violence. Unsurprisingly, many veterans avoid these celebrations, choosing instead to travel to remote locations where they do not risk being triggered by the celebratory explosions.

In these flashback moments, also known clinically as an *abreaction,* a person's body is flooded with harmful stress

---

[14] *DSM-5–TR,* 303.
[15] Van der Kolk, *The Body Keeps the Score,* 66.

hormones as though they were being assaulted again. When those suffering from PTSD are triggered into reliving their trauma, they are not merely being reminded of the past event. Traumatic flashbacks are not just frightening and vivid memories. It would be more accurate to say that the traumatic event is pulled from the past and brought back into the present, where it is no less real and violent than the day it originally happened. During traumatic flashbacks, a person relives the violence and reexperiences the emotions and physical reactions that accompanied the violence. Or, to use language that is common to Catholic sacramental theology, a flashback is the *real presence* of trauma.

Flashbacks are involuntary and intrusive, causing both emotional and physiological distress. A person who is triggered into a flashback may lose all awareness of the present reality (dissociation) and begin behaving as though they have been transported geographically and chronologically back into the traumatic event that threatened their life. These moments can be triggered by any bodily experience that recalls the past violence: the smell of smoke, the touch of someone's hand, the sound of laughter, or the simple sight of a priest's white collar. Everyday, seemingly innocuous moments easily become the impetus for terror and pain.

In *Truth and Repair: How Trauma Survivors Envision Justice*, Judith Herman recounts a story told by a sexual-assault survivor named Dr. Alissa Ackerman. She describes her experience of dissociation triggered by pleasant moments with her children: "I have a beautiful life now, but I still have PTSD. I can't wrestle on the floor with my kids. If my child jumps on me, I can't feel my body."[16] Here, Ackerman is describing

---

[16] Judith L. Herman, *Truth and Repair: How Trauma Survivors Envision Justice* (London: Basic Books, 2023), 186.

a dissociative flashback. She becomes numb to her current surroundings and instead relives the emotions and sensations of her assault. For people suffering from PTSD, such as Ackerman, beautiful life experiences like playing with one's children can be transformed into scenes of violence as flashbacks are triggered and the previous trauma is relived. In the words of van der Kolk:

> These reactions are irrational and largely outside people's control. Intense and barely controllable urges and emotions make people feel crazy—and makes them feel they don't belong to the human race. Feeling numb during birthday parties for your kids or in response to the death of a loved one makes people feel like monsters. As a result, shame becomes the dominant emotion and hiding the truth the central preoccupation.[17]

The insidious nature of PTSD can transform beautiful and sacred events into experiences of terrifying trauma. Living with PTSD means going through life not knowing when the smallest gesture, symbol, or comment will bring your world to a terrifying halt. As a result, people coping with PTSD often avoid anything that might remind them of the trauma and trigger a flashback.

> Flashbacks and reliving are in some ways worse than the trauma itself. A traumatic event has a beginning and an end—at some point it is over. But for people with PTSD, a flashback can occur at any time, whether they are awake or asleep. There is no way of knowing when it's going to occur again or how long it will last. People

---

[17] Van der Kolk, *The Body Keeps the Score*, 67.

who suffer from flashbacks often reorganize their lives around trying to protect against them.[18]

This avoidant behavior has long-lasting cognitive results, including regular negative emotional states (for example, anger, anxiety, fear), being socially disconnected, and having reduced interest in everyday life. Recall Ackerman saying "I can't wrestle on the floor with my kids." The repeated experience of flashbacks causes a person to avoid triggers. Ackerman needs to avoid these playful moments with her kids, just as military veterans are forced to avoid patriotic celebrations of the country they served. In addition to the pain and suffering that a flashback brings, avoidance behaviors often rob survivors of communities and experiences that offer fulfillment and joy.

Though our description of the symptoms of PTSD is far from exhaustive, the *DSM-5–TR* makes clear that the "clinical picture" of people suffering from PTSD is not consistent itself. Each individual will present a unique array of these symptoms:

> The clinical presentation of PTSD varies. In some individuals, fear-based reexperiencing, emotional, and behavioral symptoms may predominate. In others, anhedonic or dysphoric mood states and negative cognitions may be most prominent. In some other individuals, arousal and reactive-externalizing symptoms are prominent, while in yet others, dissociative symptoms predominate. Finally, some individuals exhibit combinations of these symptom patterns.[19]

We have chosen to focus our attention on flashbacks because they play a more acute role in subverting the way the liturgy

---

[18] Van der Kolk, 67.
[19] *DSM-5–TR*, 306.

is intended to have a positive effect on worshipers. We turn now to an examination of how these symptoms can affect a person's experience of the liturgy.

PTSD Subverting Liturgical Efficacy

Given the preceding descriptions of PTSD, it is not hard to imagine that the dynamic and stimuli-rich liturgical life of a parish community could present a challenging context for someone struggling with PTSD. This is exceedingly true when a person's PTSD is the result of sexual assault carried out by a member of the clergy. When one begins to understand the horrific nature of flashbacks, it becomes easy to understand why anyone experiencing PTSD as a result of CPSA might be eager to disaffiliate from the Church and avoid any proximity to its liturgical life.

In the second chapter we pointed out that liturgical symbols work by communicating God's love and inviting the worshipers into a life of loving friendship with God. To fully appreciate the way that PTSD can transform the liturgical symbols into symbols of violence, we must recognize that, due to the nature of flashbacks and similar "intrusion symptoms," any aspect of the liturgy can become the communication of violence. A stained-glass window, the priest's vestments, the lyrics of a hymn, the smell of wine, or any other minute aspect of the liturgy can trigger intrusive flashbacks. We find one example of this in the testimony of Dr. Deborah Rodriguez, a woman who experienced CPSA as a young child: "I could no longer see Jesus in the Catholic Church, particularly in priests. Those Roman collars the priests wore were reminders of exactly who inflicted so much pain on me and on so many others."[20] For

---

[20] Deborah Rodriguez, "MGN: A Ministry to Survivors," Maria Goretti Network: Testimonials (2024).

Rodriguez, the guilt or innocence of the man behind the collar is irrelevant. The sight of the collar itself triggers intrusive reexperiences of the abuse.

In a similar story a Catholic presbyter recounted to us how a woman, after seeing him dressed in his clerical collar and black clothing, refused to board a plane. She was terrified to be trapped on a plane with a Catholic priest. The sight of his clothing triggered such an intense reaction that she could not bring herself to get on the plane.[21] In the context of a flashback this fear cannot be reasoned away. It is not enough to assure them of their safety. It is not enough to apologize for the pain they have endured. Someone with PTSD cannot simply forgive and forget. Flashbacks and avoidance are involuntary responses, and, as such, they should never be interpreted as overreactions or, much worse, as choices that deserve blame. Ackerman is not a bad mother because she cannot wrestle with her children, veterans are not unpatriotic because they avoid Fourth of July celebrations, and survivors of CPSA are not bad Catholics because they stop going to Church.

Pope Benedict XVI offers another account of how PTSD subverts the efficacy of the liturgy in a letter entitled "The Church and the Scandal of Sexual Abuse." He recalls an appalling story of assault:

> A young woman who was a [former] altar server told me that the chaplain, her superior as an altar server,

---

[21] For a nuanced examination of how trauma affects the way grace is mediated and experienced, see the work of Jennifer Beste, especially "Receiving and Responding to God's Grace: A Re-Examination in Light of Trauma Theory," *Journal of the Society of Christian Ethics* 23, no. 1 (2003): 3–20; *God and the Victim: Traumatic Intrusions on Grace and Freedom* (Oxford, UK: Oxford University Press, 2007); and "Mediating God's Grace within the Context of Trauma: Implications for a Christian Response to Clergy Sexual Abuse," *Review and Expositor* 105, no. 2 (2008): 245–60.

always introduced the sexual abuse he was committing against her with the words: "This is my body which will be given up for you." It is obvious that this woman can no longer hear the very words of consecration without experiencing again all the horrific distress of her abuse.[22]

Often referred to as the words of institution, the phrase "this is my body which will be given up for you" is said aloud by the priest or bishop during the celebration of the Eucharist. These words are used to consecrate the bread, transforming it into the Body of Christ, which is then eaten by the congregation during the communion rite. When a priest says these words, he is meant to be acting as the presence of Christ for the Church. When the worshipers hear these words, it is as though they are hearing them spoken by Christ, inviting them into a deeper union with Christ and with one another. In short, these words are a central and essential part of the most important liturgical celebration of the Church. By using the words of institution during his assaults, the chaplain irrevocably corrupted the way this young woman experiences the consecration of the Eucharist.

Liturgical symbols do not work simply because they are spoken. They work because their meaning is believed and internalized by the one who hears them. Hence, the woman who was repeatedly assaulted by her superior had the very meaning of the words of consecration forever altered. Much like Ackerman no longer being able to experience wrestling with her children as a life-giving moment of love, this woman can no longer hear the intended message of Jesus's words. To repeat Benedict XVI's words, "It is obvious that this woman can no longer hear the very words of consecration without

---

[22] Pope Emeritus Benedict XVI, "Full Text of Benedict XVI Essay: 'The Church and the Scandal of Sexual Abuse,'" Catholic News Agency, 2019.

experiencing again all the horrific distress of her abuse."[23] For this woman the phrase "this is my body" has been transformed into a sentence that viscerally communicates violation and dehumanization. The bread that is consecrated by that sentence is no longer an invitation into communion with the Body of Christ. Instead, it is a trigger and a transport back into her trauma. No amount of ingesting and metabolizing the transubstantiated flesh of Jesus will undo the fact that hearing those words will bring her back into a state of being assaulted. In a physically, mentally, and spiritually real way, the Eucharist becomes the real presence of violence.

Another challenge proposed by flashbacks is that they can influence the survivors' relationship to the people and places in which they relive their trauma. When experiencing a flashback triggered by a priest's collar, the intensity and threatening nature of the emotional and physical reactions can alter that person's relationship with the man wearing the collar, even if their relationship had previously been healthy. As a result of the flashback, priests become associated with the trauma and are now capable of triggering flashbacks because they are perceived as a threat. In other words, the impact of the trauma extends beyond the symbols associated with the original assault. Because a flashback involves a surge of harmful stress hormones, the body instinctively defends itself by creating associations with the symbols that are present during the flashback. In this way the scope of a person's trauma can slowly grow as new associations are formed, creating new triggers that threaten the person's safety. Hence, when people try to minimize the gravity of the sexual-abuse crisis by pointing out that many cases of CPSA happened decades ago, they are failing to recognize that for people with PTSD their trauma is not a past event. In fact, through repeated flashbacks, their trauma

---

[23] Pope Emeritus Benedict XVI.

can increasingly become associated with liturgical symbols that may not have been involved in the original assault. As the likelihood of flashbacks increases, so does the need to avoid the liturgy. In short, traumatic events like CPSA have ripple effects that increasingly expand the scope of the damage being done.

The flashbacks and avoidance that arise as consequences of PTSD slowly degrade a person's quality of life. Van der Kolk describes the physical, mental, and spiritual ramifications of flashbacks as a process of imprisonment:

> If elements of trauma are replayed again and again, the accompanying stress hormones engrave those memories ever more deeply in the mind. Ordinary day-to-day events become less and less compelling. Not being able to deeply take in what is going on around them makes it impossible to feel fully alive. . . . Not being fully alive in the present keeps them more firmly imprisoned in the past.[24]

If the liturgy is meant to invite worshipers more fully into an active life of friendship with God (that is, to fully participate in the divine nature), then PTSD should be seen as a prison that keeps people from being fully alive. Stress hormones ingrain traumatic memories more deeply, forever resignifying the symbols of the liturgy. Furthermore, these stress hormones physiologically damage the body. Digestive issues, muscle and joint pain, and cardiac damage can all result from prolonged exposure to these hormones. Telling Catholics who are suffering from years of PTSD that they have a moral and religious obligation to attend the liturgy at least once a week shames (that is, spiritually abuses) them into experiencing both mental

---

[24] Van der Kolk, *The Body Keeps the Score*, 67.

and physical assault. Put differently, they are being kept in a prison that keeps them from flourishing as the living image of God they were made to be. When people suffer from liturgically triggered PTSD, the liturgy literally poisons the body, inflicting pain and death. For the person with PTSD, the liturgy ceases to be a *source* of grace. Due to the Church's culture of death, the person suffering from PTSD is left with a disposition that subverts liturgical efficacy. The liturgy is no longer experienced as an offer of God's grace. Instead, it is an act of violence.

Further, the Church's clericalist culture stops the liturgy from being the *summit* of grace. As worshipers suffering from PTSD avoid the parish and its liturgical community, they are excluded from the fullness of grace by their need to avoid triggers. Or more accurately, they are being excluded from the summit of grace by the traumatic abuse they continue to endure at the hands of the clericalist culture.

While PTSD does not invalidate the liturgy, it does something far worse. An invalid liturgy can still fruitfully offer grace and be a beautiful celebration of communion and salvation. However, a valid liturgy that triggers flashbacks and avoidance subverts the grace it intends to offer and offers dehumanization instead. Paraphrasing van der Kolk, CPSA flashbacks that are triggered by liturgical symbols can, in some ways, be worse than the original sexual assault. Unlike the initial trauma, these flashbacks have no beginning and no end. The liturgy becomes an ongoing assault.

Our claim that PTSD subverts liturgical efficacy by corrupting the symbolic meaning of liturgical symbols should not be controversial. Roman Catholic tradition has long held that the meaning and efficacy of sacred symbols can be influenced by their use and greater contexts. Roman Catholic officials know that, when a liturgical symbol has been desecrated by egregious abuse (that is, sacrilege), it ought not to be expected (or allowed) to function as a liturgically fruitful symbol of God's self-offering. Sacrilege is the abuse of a consecrated symbol in a manner that distorts its sacred character, rendering it null and void (that is, desecrated). When a sacred symbol is desecrated, its previous abuse becomes an irrevocable part of the history that provides its meaning. Or, to borrow an image used by liturgical theologian Layla Karst, these liturgical symbols become embroidered with abuse.[25] Many people have family heirlooms with special significance that are only used in certain circumstances. Part of what makes these heirlooms so special is that they are set apart from other items that are used on an everyday basis. A family might have a special set of dishes that is only used on special occasions to help mark the importance of the occasion while also serving as a reminder of an important event and/or relationship. A married couple might have a set of wedding china that is only used on their anniversary. If that china is used for other purposes, especially if those purposes are off-putting or antithetical to the celebration of the couple's love, then its integrity as a symbol can be compromised. This is what is meant by sacrilege and desecration.

In the Archdiocese of New Orleans in 2020, Archbishop Gregory Aymond ordered an altar to be destroyed and burned because it had been desecrated through the sexual misconduct of Fr. Travis Clark, the parish pastor.[26] This instance of desecration didn't involve any children or sexual assault. The pastor had consensual sex with two women on top of the altar, yet it

---

[25] Layla Karst, "Broken Bodies, Broken Symbols: Liturgical Ripples of the Clergy Sex Abuse Crisis," in *Harvesting and Sowing: Ministry, Protagonism, and the Laity in an Age of Epochal Change*," ed. Michael Canaris and Maureen O'Brien (Mahwah, NJ: Paulist, 2025).

[26] JD Flynn, "After 'Demonic' Desecration, New Orleans Church Reconsecrated as Details about Priest Emerge," *National Catholic Register* online, October 13, 2020.

was clear that the misconduct had rendered a powerful liturgical symbol worthy of destruction. Perhaps more accurately, the sacrilege had already destroyed the symbol's ability to function, and the physical destruction of the symbol simply completed the destruction. In addition to burning the altar, Archbishop Aymond began the process of laicization for Fr. Clark. The process of laicization removes a priest from ordained ministry. In this case it means that his conduct rendered him unable to fulfill his role as an ordained symbol of Christ. This story illustrates the fact that holy symbols can become so corrupt that they demand destruction lest they serve to corrupt other liturgical symbols that surround them. If Fr. Clark were allowed to celebrate mass on the altar where the congregation knew he had sex with two women, then that celebration of the Eucharist, while perfectly valid, would struggle to fruitfully offer the grace it was meant to communicate. When those who are experiencing PTSD as a result of CPSA distance themselves from the Catholic Church and its liturgical life, they are essentially doing what Bishop Aymond did in laicizing Fr. Clark and burning the altar. They are purging their lives of corrupt and broken symbols that are still repeatedly harming them. Instead of trying to keep people who have experienced CPSA close to these harmful symbols, what might it mean to "destroy and burn" those aspects of the clericalist culture that have abused innocent people and become the real presence of death?

Conclusion: Revealing a Culture of Death

The liturgical life of the Church is intended to be a process of cultivating grace. In the liturgy the Church is meant to encounter Christ as one who provocatively calls to us as friends. The symbols of the liturgy are supposed to be divine communication that makes Christ's love felt by those who participate.

Yet the scandal of systemic CPSA has left in its wake an untold amount of trauma and PTSD, deeply corrupting the dispositions that are necessary for the liturgy to bear fruit in the lives of worshipers.

The problem to be fixed does not lie within the people suffering from PTSD. The problem to be fixed lies solely in the Church's abusive clericalist culture that is maintained and cultivated by the liturgy. This is a difficult truth to accept. Many well-meaning Catholics believe that God is capable of anything and that the liturgy (especially the Eucharist) is the most perfect manifestation of God's omnipotent love in this life. As a result, they tend to believe that the liturgy could not possibly be a harmful activity. They see the liturgy as an incorruptible source of health and healing. In this way they see the liturgy as a divine act of *dispensing* grace. This attitude is an example of clericalism insofar as it overemphasizes the liturgy as a *source* of grace. In short, the liturgy is not a special category of activity that somehow transcends the rules of our human bodies. The liturgy is not a sacred vending machine that fruitfully dispenses grace regardless of who is participating. The dispositions of the worshipers matter.

The majority of clergy know that they should never knowingly encourage someone suffering from PTSD to attend the liturgy. However, the majority of Catholics also fail to appreciate the prevalence of such trauma in the life of the Church. Pastors should not assume their parishioners are healthy until otherwise informed. Every congregation includes people who are struggling with PTSD, and it would be safe to assume that the Catholic Church's history of CPSA has led to the widespread erosion of liturgical efficacy. Roman Catholics, especially those in leadership positions, must recognize and accept the fact that, for many survivors of CPSA, aspects of Catholic culture and tradition that many Catholics have grown to love (for example, clerical clothing, the words of institution, crucifixes, and so on) have been transformed into the real presence of violence.

Within the culture of clericalism, the purpose of the liturgy is to maintain the clergy's power and the laity's deference. If this is true, then we can expect those in power to demand that the laity participate in the liturgy regardless of their trauma. For the ordained men benefiting from the clericalist culture of death, the liturgy is wielded as a tool used to maintain ownership of and control over their sheep.

Tragically, the majority of abusers, whether pastors, parents, or spouses, truly believe that they are doing what is best for their victims and that they are acting out of love. Yet, we know that nothing could be further from the truth. Well-intentioned abuse is still violence and abuse. Indeed, an argument could be made that well-intentioned abuse is more damaging precisely because it sells itself as motivated by care and love. Abuse that comes from overt malice is easier to recognize as abuse. A culture of consistent abuse that is presented as love ends up teaching people to confuse abuse for love. In the context of clericalism, a lay person learns to see deference and self-sacrifice as acts of piety and devotion to God, when, in reality, this behavior is abusive and dehumanizing.

Too often, the Church's response to the scandal of systemic CPSA has been to treat the symptoms. Well-intentioned apologies, monetary payouts to survivors, and new policies aimed at protecting children are all helpful steps that can contribute to the long-term healing of those harmed by CPSA. Obviously, people suffering from PTSD deserve care and support as they seek to heal and move forward with their lives. However, we have not examined PTSD and its effects on liturgical efficacy in order to cast it as a fixable problem. We cannot reiterate enough that the problem does not lie within the people suffering from PTSD. Their pain and suffering are symptoms of a greater disease. We focus on the consequences of systemic CPSA so that we can come to a deeper understanding of the cultural causes of the abuse. Trauma, PTSD, and flashbacks are all revelatory moments in the crucified Body of Christ. We must hear the testimonies of those who have suffered CPSA so that we can know the source of their pain and purge it from the Church.

4

Losing Faith

Moral Injury and the Liturgy

> *"Tell them . . . what he took from me. Not just my innocence but my faith. I'm like a spiritual orphan, betrayed by what I loved, and I feel lost and alone."*
>
> —"Danny"[1]

Post-traumatic stress disorder (PTSD) is by no means the only consequence of trauma. This chapter explores moral injury and highlights how moral injury, too, can have devastating effects on the liturgical life of the Church. As PTSD is capable of subverting liturgical efficacy, rendering the liturgy unable to serve fruitfully as the source and summit of grace, moral injury is a condition that can hinder the liturgy's ability to communicate the love of God in a fruitful manner. Resulting from a deep sense of betrayal, moral injury shakes a person's faith to such an extent that their sense of self and sense of the world begins to crumble. The trust and love that someone may have once

---

[1] Joseph J. Guido, "A Unique Betrayal: Clergy Sexual Abuse in the Context of the Catholic Religious Tradition," *Journal of Child Sexual Abuse* 17, no. 3–4 (2008): 257.

had toward the Church falters. In the wake of moral injury, the liturgy can stir up feelings of betrayal and pain, ultimately hindering its ability to offer grace and provoke love. The goal of the liturgy is to form moral agents who live lives of faith, hope, and love that are expressed through active communion with one another and with the world. In other words, the liturgy should build up one's sense of agency and allow worshipers to live as Christ lived. As we will see, *moral injury* is a term used to describe various conditions that erode one's agency, leaving behind a person who struggles to find meaning and purpose in life. Therefore, moral injury, like PTSD, is a corruption of the predispositions necessary for the liturgy to be fruitful in a person's life.

What Is Moral Injury?

As a concept, moral injury provides us with the framework to begin to understand how betrayals at personal and institutional levels can undermine individuals' sense of self while simultaneously damaging their ability to make sense of the world around them. According to moral theologian Marcus Mescher, the term *injury* is used "to make visible the psychological turmoil and spiritual struggle that can never be totally externalized," while also signaling that, like other injuries, healing and recovery are possible.[2] So, how does betrayal *injure* a person? Further, how does that injury end up becoming so destabilizing?

To illustrate the depth of turmoil experienced by those who have moral injury, one need only to read the testimony of individuals who endured the betrayal central to clergy

---

[2] Marcus Mescher, "Toward a Taxonomy of Moral Injury: Confronting the Harm Caused by Clergy Sexual Abuse," *Journal of the Society of Christian Ethics* 43, no. 1 (2023): 77.

perpetrated sexual abuse (CPSA).[3] Dr. Scott Easton, Danielle Leone-Sheehan, RN, and Dr. Patrick O'Leary conducted one of the first large-scale studies of adult male individuals who experienced CPSA from childhood, paying particular attention to how such betrayals affected their self-identity over the long term. A participant recounted the crisis of self-identity as a result of CPSA: "I started realizing its effect on me about 10 years ago. The 'self-identity' I carried for 35 years was a lie. I do not believe I have developed a 'new' one yet."[4] Within this statement the individual expresses symptoms often included within definitions of moral injury, particularly the hindered ability to find meaning, leading to a feeling that their self-identity was a lie and the stunted ability to feel as though they even have a true self-identity. As within the context of Easton, Leone-Sheehan, and O'Leary's study, the experience of CPSA directly undermined this man's self-identity.

Alongside a sense of meaninglessness, the undermining of agency is central to the definition of moral injury and echoed in a statement by another participant within the study. In conversation specifically about self-harming behaviors, the participant described the feeling of powerlessness and loss of agency:

> It was like being in a totally dark room and someone or something in that room keeps hurting you but you can't see where the pain is coming from, you can't protect yourself. You try everything you can think of, but each

---

[3] We feel it necessary to note that these testimonies are only snippets of an individual's full recollection. Within these statements we see central themes, however, and intend to make clear that a mere phrase can never fully do justice to an individual's lived experience as a whole.

[4] Scott D. Easton, Danielle M. Leone-Sheehan, and Patrick J. O'Leary, "'I Will Never Know the Person Who I Could Have Become': Perceived Change in Self-Identity Among Adult Survivors of Clergy-Perpetrated Sexual Abuse," *Journal of Interpersonal Violence* 34, no. 6 (2019): 1147.

solution only causes you more pain. You come to feel that you are not even real, you are this big cosmic joke and the only way to stop the joke is to end your life.[5]

Within this testimony we witness a profound undermining of agency. The participant's agency to even survive feels out of his control, as he feels that he cannot protect himself from the pressures of suicidal ideation. He describes a continued feeling of vulnerability and lack of safety, resulting from the violence of CPSA.

Fr. Joseph J. Guido, a Catholic priest and professor of psychology, interviewed an individual referred to as Danny in his article "A Unique Betrayal: Clergy Sexual Abuse in the Context of the Catholic Religious Tradition."[6] Fr. Guido contextualized the conversation with Danny, writing that when they first met, Danny "had not seen the inside of a Catholic church in two decades, nor had he spoken with a Catholic priest in that time. We met in a coffee shop, 'neutral turf' as Danny had called it."[7] Guido notes that the conversation was a result of a therapist suggesting that telling his story to a priest might be therapeutic, as Danny hoped his story might help others. In their conversation, spanning two hours, Danny insisted, "Tell them . . . what he took from me. Not just my innocence but my faith. I'm like a spiritual orphan, betrayed by what I loved, and I feel lost and alone."[8] Danny's statement provides a direct example of the overlap between moral injury and liturgical efficacy, for he expresses that his faith was undermined. Beyond his faith, his continued feelings of being lost and alone are symptoms congruent with those of moral injury. A sense of having endured damage to one's identity is common to

---

[5] Easton, Leone-Sheehan, and O'Leary, 1149.
[6] Guido, "A Unique Betrayal," 256.
[7] Guido, 256.
[8] Guido, 257.

each of these testimonials. Feeling lost, empty, or like a fraud, CPSA left them feeling that their abuse robbed them of their identity, leaving them unsure of who they are in relation to the rest of the world.

In contrast to PTSD, moral injury is not currently a medical diagnosis in the *DSM*. Yet, its prevalence as a concept that is used to better understand and describe the pain of people suffering from trauma has been increasing since the 1990s, when the term was first used. Originally used as a way to describe the experience of soldiers who had perceived a betrayal from their military leaders, the term *moral injury* was coined in 1995 by clinical psychiatrist Jonathan Shay. According to Brett Litz and Patricia Kerig, in their article "Introduction to the Special Issue on Moral Injury," Shay used the term to describe his observation of "the psychic, social, and cultural struggles war veterans face as they try to regain a sense of trust after being betrayed by leaders in combat."[9] According to Shay himself, moral injury is a "betrayal of 'what's right' by someone who holds legitimate authority in a 'high-stakes' situation."[10] For example, when soldiers carry out an order from their commanding officer to commit an unwarranted, unjust act of violence, they may come to feel that their trust in their leader was betrayed. Having previously believed in the moral righteousness of their military efforts and in the virtue of their leaders, they are now left doubting their own sense of right and wrong and the values that gave their life a sense of meaning and purpose. The authority to whom they dedicated their life has been compromised. Because betrayal compromises a person's attachments to their sources of authority and safety, inflicting

---

[9] Brett T. Litz and Patricia K. Kerig, "Introduction to the Special Issue on Moral Injury: Conceptual Challenges, Methodological Issues, and Clinical Applications," *Journal of Traumatic Stress*, no. 32 (2019): 341.

[10] Jonathan Shay, *Achilles in Vietnam: Combat Trauma and the Undoing of Character* (New York: Simon and Schuster, 1995), 208.

shame, fear, and doubt, it injures them in a way that "impacts meaning-making and intensifies the sense of injustice."[11]

While PTSD is often characterized by intense feelings of fear and helplessness, Mescher points out that psychologists often describe moral injury as accompanied by feelings of guilt, shame, and anger.[12] To illustrate this distinction, recall Dr. Ackerman's experience of PTSD flashbacks when wrestling with her children that were described in the previous chapter.[13] When her child jumped on her back, her body became numb and she was filled with intense fear. A beautiful experience with her family was transformed into the presence of violence. Contrast Ackerman's account with this account from an adult struggling with moral injury as a result of childhood CPSA:

> Every potential opportunity to commit suicide was fantasized about, jumping in a fire, jumping off a cliff, driving into a semi-truck, shooting myself, hanging myself. . . . I fought this down all my life, so what does that say about my self-identity— I feel like I didn't have one, except to try and control my suicidalness, anger, and depression.[14]

Rather than the intrusive experiences of intense fear and pain that accompany PTSD, the pain of moral injury is a persistent sense of meaninglessness, anger, and depression. The anguish

---

[11] Easton, Leone-Sheehan, and O'Leary, "'I Will Never Know the Person Who I Could Have Become,'" 1156.

[12] Mescher, "Toward a Taxonomy of Moral Injury," 80.

[13] Judith L. Herman, *Truth and Repair: How Trauma Survivors Envision Justice* (London: Basic Books, 2023), 186.

[14] Easton, Leone-Sheehan, and O'Leary, "'I Will Never Know the Person Who I Could Have Become,'" 1149.

inflicted by moral injury can destroy the ability to find purpose and meaning in life. As a result, suicidal ideation can become a persistent threat.

When an authority figure (for example, a parent, a political leader, a pastor, and so on) acts in a manner that violates the trust that has been given to them, they inflict damage on the system of attachments that a person uses to construct an identity (that is, their place and role in the world). If a child grows up in a household where their grandparents are their primary caregivers, then that person develops attachments whereby they trust the grandparents to love them, provide for them, and protect them. That child, then, develops a sense of self in which they understand themselves in terms of their attachments to the grandparents. Their sense of self-worth and purpose is derived from the experience of being loved and cared for by their grandparents. Additionally, the child's worldview is constructed based on the experience of the grandparents' care. They begin to see the world as a just place where humans have dignity and value, where love and kindness lead to happiness and flourishing. If, then, one of those grandparents begins to behave contrary to the love and care they are supposed to be providing, this constitutes a betrayal that violates the trust of the child. The result is a deterioration of the attachments that provided meaning. The child's self-worth begins to be called into question, and their sense of a just world gives way to a sense of danger and chaos. In a real sense, the child goes through a prolonged and painful loss of self precisely because the culture and community in which they placed their trust has been taken away by betrayal. When a person loses their culture and community, the result is a sense of loneliness and emptiness, as we saw in the previously cited quotes from CPSA survivors. The experience of having one's identity destabilized is often described by phrases such as a "shattered self" and a "shattered worldview."[15] Like a refugee who is violently displaced from their home, taken away from the language, food, architecture, and other cultural symbols that have formed their identity, someone experiencing moral injury often feels abandoned and isolated, unable to make intimate connections with themselves, their community, or their God.

PTSD and moral injury are not mutually exclusive, nor are they necessarily co-occurring. Instead, they are two psychological phenomena that can be the result of the same event or set of events, but they differ in the actual symptoms and criteria. Psychologists argue that moral injury allows for more inclusion than does PTSD. Litz and Kerig remark that PTSD has been "historically framed as a danger and victimization-based disorder" whose diagnosis requires "the experience to have been a direct or indirect exposure to life-threat or sexual violence."[16] In other words, PTSD is a category that is focused on victims and witnesses of acute violence. Moral injury, on the other hand, is a broader concept that focuses on the psychological effects that acts of betrayal can have on perpetrators, enablers, victims, bystanders, and witnesses. Because it can apply to these different types of people, moral injury provides a framework that can help analysts examine the multifaceted complexity of the Catholic sex-abuse scandal. For example, a member of the laity may not have been directly assaulted by a member of the clergy, yet they may still feel symptoms of moral injury due to feeling betrayed by authority figures they once trusted. Moral injury allows for a critical examination of the moral consequences that a culture of clericalism may have upon the individuals affiliated with and exposed to this abusive environment.

---

[15] Michelle Panchuk, "The Shattered Spiritual Self: A Philosophical Exploration of Religious Trauma," *Res Philosophica* 95, no. 3 (2018): 509.

[16] Litz and Kerig, "Introduction to the Special Issue on Moral Injury," 342–44.

Given this general description of moral injury, we turn now to an examination of the different types of moral injury that can arise as a result of different types of betrayal. While interest in moral injury has reached beyond the treating of war trauma and become an increasingly popular point of discussion wherever abuse is being studied, there remains a lack of an agreed-upon, empirical "gold standard" for the term, preventing the phenomenon from being a clinical diagnosis.[17] To use Mescher's phrase, moral injury is very much "a concept in development."[18] Hence, we have chosen to avoid providing a single definition out of respect for the ongoing nature of psychological research. Instead, we offer a description of moral injury that allows us to recognize, describe, and analyze the impact that systemic CPSA has had on the members of the Catholic Church.

Different Types of Moral Injury

Betrayal can occur in many forms. As such, moral injury can result from different events and manifest in diverse ways. Just as the same event may be traumatic for one person but not traumatic for another, an event that results in moral injury for one person will not necessarily mean that everyone exposed to that same event will experience moral injury. The context of a relationship and the intensity of the trust have an impact on if and how moral injury manifests. Hence, we can say that moral injury exists on a spectrum.

For example, there can be significant differences between how a perpetrator who freely used their agency to harm another person experiences moral injury and how a victim whose agency was taken away and whose trust was betrayed

---

[17] Litz and Kerig, 342.
[18] Mescher, "Toward a Taxonomy of Moral Injury," 86.

will experience moral injury. In this section we rely on Mescher's taxonomy of moral injury, which includes five categories of moral injury: (1) actions I did to another, (2) another's actions toward me, (3) failure to act, (4) institutional affiliation, and (5) exposure to a toxic environment.[19] To assist in understanding these categories, we provide a secular example and follow that with an example related to the CPSA crisis, including narrative illustrations.

Actions I Did to Another

The first type of moral injury accounts for the ability of perpetrators to experience powerful symptoms such as guilt, erosion of self, and deep shame. Because this category describes moral injury caused by one's agency, it is referred to as *perpetration-based* moral injury, in contrast to *betrayal-based* moral injury.[20] However, one could argue that the experience of intense shame at having violated one's own moral code is a type of betrayal of one's self. Moral failures challenge a person's self-perception, confronting them with difficult truths about their moral character. Put differently, it is possible for a person to violate the trust that they have in themselves. This type of moral injury could be experienced by an individual who made the choice to drive under the influence of alcohol or drugs, causing an accident that resulted in the death of an innocent person. They may experience moral injury, resulting in feelings of extreme guilt and shame, causing their perception of self to change drastically and leave them, as soldiers have described, as if their souls are "in anguish" and are "eaten alive" by the recognition of the harm that they inflicted on others. As a result, such persons may no longer trust themselves and

---

[19] Mescher, 85–91.
[20] Mescher, 86.

may struggle to see themselves as good, valuable, or worthy of forgiveness and love.

In the context of systemic CPSA, this form of moral injury could be experienced by those who committed sexual abuse, leaders who ordered others to hide the abuse, or individuals who played a role in enabling the abuse to continue. For example, there are examples of clergy who died by suicide as they were awaiting trial for credible allegations of CPSA.[21] Of course, not all perpetrators experience this form of moral injury. As Mescher points out, "Those who suffer from narcissism or refuse to acknowledge the harm they caused—like many priest abusers who deny survivors of clergy sexual abuse remorse or repentance—would likely fail to demonstrate symptoms of moral injury."[22] Far from a coincidence, factors such as narcissism and a lack of accountability tend to mirror the type of ordained minister cultivated by clericalism, perhaps helping to explain why evidence of remorse and accountability is, while minimally present, ultimately lacking.

Another's Actions toward Me

The second category of moral injury is often referred to as *betrayal-based* moral injury, because an individual in a position of authority violates the trust of another by doing something cruel and harmful. This type of moral injury is most closely linked to experiencing directly or witnessing trauma and can often accompany other symptoms of PTSD. As such, this is often the most acute form of moral injury, resulting in the

---

[21] Walter Sánchez Silva, "French Priest Accused of Abusing a Young Girl Commits Suicide," *Catholic News Agency* online, July 17, 2023; Daniel Payne, "New Mexico Priest Dies by Suicide amid Child Sex Abuse Investigation," *National Catholic Register* online, May 28, 2024.

[22] Mescher, "Toward a Taxonomy of Moral Injury," 87.

erosion of an individual's identity, beliefs, and sense of self. This particular type of moral injury is particularly corrosive and is "cognitive, affective, and embodied,"[23] creating an impediment to emotional, relational, mental, and, of particular note in our context, spiritual development for an individual.

For example, consider the case of Dr. Larry Nassar. Nassar is a prime example of the type of trusted individual whose betrayal can destroy a person's sense of trust. Nassar was viewed as a respected doctor in the sport of gymnastics. Throughout his career he published articles and created training for other sports-medicine specialists. He was employed by Team USA and Michigan State University as team doctor. While serving in this capacity he was sexually abusing the patients under his care.[24] Megan Halicek, who was fifteen when she was abused by Nassar, stated in court that she viewed him as an "absolute God." She believed: "He was the only one that could help me. . . . He gave me hope. Here I was, a scared little girl in excruciating back pain. This grown man confidently offered me salvation, healing freedom."[25] Ashley Erickson remarked: "I have to rethink everything. I have no trust left. How can I trust when someone I trusted for years took advantage of me?"[26] The testimony from Nassar's court case depicts the depth of pain for those experiencing this type of moral injury. Those who experienced abuse at the hands of Nassar experienced impeded development, were left with a hindered ability to trust others, and, in the case of Chelsea Markham, were led to drug

---

[23] Mescher, 87.

[24] A. Wellman, M. B. Meitl, P. Kinkade, and A. Huffman, "Routine Activities Theory as a Formula for Systematic Sexual Abuse: A Content Analysis of Survivors' Testimony Against Larry Nassar," *American Journal of Criminal Justice* 46, no. 2 (2021), 318–21.

[25] Sarah Biddlecombe, "Powerful Stories from the Women Who Confronted Predator Larry Nassar," *Stylist* online, November 2017.

[26] Biddlecombe.

abuse, depression, and, eleven years after the abuse, suicide at the age of twenty-three.[27]

When this type of betrayal occurs at the hands of a Catholic priest, who is meant to represent Jesus, the repercussions can be devastating, rupturing the person's relationship with themselves, their loved ones, their community, and with God. Because clerics are meant to serve as symbols of Christ and live a life emblematic of Jesus's life, their abuse constitutes "a betrayal of the sacramental meaning of his authority."[28] In the wake of CPSA, adult survivors recall the devastation such abuse had on their self-image as a child of God and the hope they had for the future. Participants within Easton's qualitative analysis expressed the extreme shame they felt from being abused by a priest, remarking that they "spent a lot of time thinking I was going to hell," with others feeling they were "inherently damaged goods" and believing they were "less of a person" than those around them.[29] Recall Danny's testimony, wherein he emphasized that the abuser took from him, "Not just my innocence but my faith," leaving him, "a spiritual orphan, betrayed by what I loved, [feeling] lost and alone."[30] Among a multitude of individual accounts in other studies and countless message-board posts in CPSA groups, Catholic sexual abuse left those affected feeling empty, lost spiritually and emotionally, with little hope for their future.

Failure to Act

Mescher's third category describes moral injury that arises from a failure to stop or attempt to stop harm being done.

---

[27] Biddlecombe.
[28] Guido, "A Unique Betrayal," 257–58.
[29] Easton, Leone-Sheehan, and O'Leary, "'I Will Never Know the Person Who I Could Have Become,'" 1148–50.
[30] Guido, "A Unique Betrayal," 257.

This category is most helpful because it brings nuance to the overly simplistic binary of perpetrator and victim. By considering those who have failed to act, one can include all "implicated subjects" who "fail to exercise their moral duty to protect others."[31] For example, this could be the result of having prior knowledge of a threat and not pursuing recourse to prevent said actions. If an individual heard another's plans to commit violence against a group of people or in a public setting and failed to report to authorities or take such comments seriously, they may experience moral injury due to their internalized guilt and shame over knowing ahead of time and failing to take action.

In the context of systemic CPSA, this form of moral injury is likely among the most common experiences for Catholics. Since most Catholics have not been directly assaulted or witnessed any assault, their sense of betrayal comes from an awareness of bishops and other Catholic leaders who failed to use their power to protect others from harm. As we emphasized in the second chapter, the enormity of the scandal lies not just in the number of people who have been abused but in knowing the extent of the willful cover-up of the abuse. When Catholics discover that their bishop had known about a perpetrator and failed to report them to authorities or had allowed the predator to go about their ministerial duties without interference, their trust in their bishop has been betrayed, and they are at risk of suffering this form of moral injury. If an ordained minister's sacred duty is to protect his congregation and he fails to do so, then the priest may feel that he has enabled or perpetuated a grave transgression against his moral beliefs and conscience.

---

[31] Mescher, "Toward a Taxonomy of Moral Injury," 87–88.

Institutional Affiliation

Moral injury that results from institutional affiliation draws our attention directly to the cultural and social aspects of moral injury. In contrast to previously discussed categories, this type of moral injury occurs when an organizational culture harms an individual's sense of self and identity writ large. Although more diffused than the first and second categories, this type of moral injury still cuts to extreme depths as an individual experiences pain and hurt based upon their connection to an organization's entire belief system, often an organization that plays a major factor in defining their identity.

Mescher describes the moral injury that soldiers may develop as result of their shared experience of basic training, wherein they are desensitized to violence and their identity has been "incorporated into a unit that has normalized so many vicious views and habits."[32] This type of moral injury does not necessitate that soldiers be particularly engaged in violence or actions that violate their own moral code. However, due to the fusion of their identity with their unit that is accomplished during their basic training, soldiers can come to "recognize harm done to them by an institution, not just by an individual."[33]

In the context of CPSA, Thomas Doyle, an ex-priest and whistleblower, displays moral injury resulting from institutional affiliation as he recounts his experience witnessing the grave failure of the Catholic Church to respond to widespread abuse it was keenly aware of. Doyle recalls:

> As I was drawn deeper and deeper into the total phenomenon of clergy sexual abuse I began to experience

---
[32] Mescher, 88.
[33] Mescher, 88

a deep and gnawing pain that I eventually learned was fundamentally spiritual in nature. From the outset of my experience in the mid to late 1980's I found it emotionally jarring as I saw the broad-based dishonesty and callousness of Church leaders. At first I could not believe what I thought I was seeing and it was only with intense emotional and spiritual pain that I finally accepted the reality of what I saw before me . . . the bishops were more concerned about themselves and hardly concerned about the victims. The radical incongruity between the response of the institutional Church to the entire clergy sexual-abuse phenomenon and to the victims and the Church's dogged concern for orthodoxy and doctrinal integrity remains a profound mystery for me.[34]

Doyle's experience of betrayal highlights the erosive nature that moral injury has on an individual, when their expectations, based upon their institution's belief system, are violated. Doyle further describes his journey leaving the Catholic Church as he was able to push past a state of denial and "connect this denial with my own dependence on the Catholic 'system' of security."[35]

Exposure to a Toxic Environment

Mescher describes the final category of moral injury as "the most diffuse, analogous to thirdhand smoke."[36] When exposed to a toxic environment, individuals can feel a sense of vulner-

---

[34] Thomas P. Doyle, "The Spiritual Trauma Experienced by Victims of Sexual Abuse by Catholic Clergy," *Pastoral Psychology* (2009), 257–58.

[35] Doyle, "The Spiritual Trauma Experienced by Victims of Sexual Abuse by Catholic Clergy," 239–60.

[36] Mescher, "Toward a Taxonomy of Moral Injury," 90.

ability and moral violation from an event that they may not have directly witnessed or perpetrated. To suffer from this type of moral injury, one needs to be exposed to an environment marked by a culture of violence and abuse. In the twenty-first century, wherein nationalism and patriotism are pivotal to the identity of some global citizens, living within a given nation as a cause for exposure-based moral injury is a live option. For example, the United States heavily emphasizes its citizens being "Americans," pledging allegiance to only their country on a consistent basis and portraying itself as the "greatest nation on earth." Many American citizens' moral conscience is slowly degraded through exposure to escalating xenophobia, misogyny, and racism. Even if they have not witnessed overt acts of oppression, they can experience moral injury that arises from exposure to a toxic culture as they are slowly deformed by the culture's moral bankruptcy. When a person is constantly surrounded by immorality, they are at risk of adopting that very immorality.

In the context of systemic CPSA, this form of moral injury arises as Catholics live their lives immersed in what Pope Francis has called the clericalist culture of death. On one hand, the Church presents itself as a culture of love and justice, where God's grace and friendship are offered through the celebration of the liturgy. On the other hand, these values are betrayed by the clear presence of a clericalist culture that denigrates the laity and uses them as a means to idolize and empower the clergy. Even without realizing it, a Catholic's morals and sense of self can be slowly eroded by the consistent betrayal that is experienced by living within a clericalist culture that is the antithesis of the gospel message.

Each of the five categories of moral injury described by Mescher provides a lens for understanding the large-scale betrayals that continue to occur through systemic CPSA.

A global event as widespread and prolonged as the Roman Catholic sexual-abuse crisis will certainly include all of these types of moral injury. In fact, before turning to a discussion of how moral injury hinders liturgical efficacy, we would like to address one more type of moral injury: "sacred moral injury."[37]

Sacred Moral Injury

As described by psychiatrist Len Sperry, sacred moral injury is essentially a combination of the second, third, and fourth categories described above: another's actions toward me, failure to act, and institutional affiliation. According to Sperry:

> [Sacred moral injury] involves both a personal moral failure and a systemic moral failure. The personal moral failure is by the abuser-betrayer. The systemic moral failure is by the religious organization that is complicit with the abuse. To fully comprehend the concept of sacred moral injury, it is essential to understand that the abuser's immoral behavior is somehow sanctioned or condoned by the religious organization.[38]

In other words, sacred moral injury is unique because it (1) occurs within a religious context and is the result of compounding betrayals; (2) is a personal betrayal; and (3) is an institutional betrayal. When a Catholic priest who has been formed by a clericalist culture abuses someone and is then protected by the hierarchy and allowed to continue abusing others, the situation is ripe for sacred moral injury. The possible results of this

---

[37] Len Sperry, "Moral Injury in Christian Organizations: Sacred Moral Injury," in *Christianity and Psychiatry*, ed. John R. Peteet, H. Steven Moffic, Ahmed Hankir, and Harold G. Koenig (Cham, Switzerland: Springer International Publishing AG, 2021), 113–27.

[38] Sperry, "Moral Injury in Christian Organizations," 116.

unique form of moral injury are similar to the other categories of moral injury: loss of trust, anger, despair, suicidality, erosion of one's identity, and difficulty finding meaning and purpose in life. However, sacred moral injury has a particularly acute impact on one's faith and spirituality.

Sacred moral injury harms individuals' relationship with their religious community and with God. In other words, their sources of meaning are compromised. When Catholics are taught to place their trust in clergy as though they were the very embodiments of God's loving authority, their trust takes on a sacred quality. It is no longer just a matter of trusting another human being, but entrusting one's spiritual well-being to someone who is perceived as acting in God's name. Sperry summarizes this impact bluntly: "The abused may reframe their sexual assault by a priest or minister as 'God raped me.'"[39] Hence, sacred moral injury damages one's relationship with self, religious community, and God. In essence, sacred moral injury alienates the person from that which gives meaning to their life.[40] The impact of sacred moral injury is profound, as it touches upon the very core of one's spiritual identity. This type of moral injury can cause an internal crisis, wherein individuals struggle to reconcile their shattered beliefs with their lived experiences. In short, the myriad betrayals perpetrated by systemic CPSA inflict serious injury on the Church's membership, greatly hindering their ability to live up to their identity as children of God and followers of Christ.

Moral Injury Hindering Liturgical Efficacy

How, then, do these forms of moral injury affect the fruitfulness of the liturgy? In the previous chapter we saw that

---

[39] Sperry, 119.
[40] Sperry, 115.

flashbacks can cause liturgical symbols to become the "real presence" of violence instead of being an offering of God's love. As such, the flashbacks associated with PTSD subvert liturgical efficacy by turning it into an act of dehumanizing violence that survivors of CPSA rightly avoid. Moral injury, on the other hand, is less intense insofar as it does not involve an intrusive reliving of one's trauma. As we pointed out above, not all moral injury is the result of a personal experience of trauma. Instead, moral injury erodes the trust that is necessary for liturgical symbols to fruitfully communicate their intended meaning. This corruption of the logic of the liturgy's symbolic framework is primarily accomplished due to the central role played by the ordained minister. Because ordained ministers play a conceptually and physically central role in the liturgy, how they are perceived has a deep impact on how the rest of the liturgical symbols are interpreted.

> The ordination of a man to the priesthood is no mere deputation or conveyance of office but something that radically changes him. In this sense, the priest-perpetrator is not only a trusted and honored figure but is by virtue of ordination an *alter Christus*, another Christ, and his betrayal of that trust and dishonoring of that role cannot be separated from his sacramental character and meaning. Indeed, precisely because Catholicism suffuses the created order with added meaning, the violation of that order—the violation of an adolescent's body, or of a church or its sacristy—is also a violation of the meaning that it is meant to convey.[41]

In other words, what a member of the priesthood does deeply affects how the rest of the priests are seen by the laity and by

---

[41] Guido, "A Unique Betrayal," 257.

the rest of the world. When someone is badly bitten by a dog, it is not strange when they become wary of all dogs. Likewise, when a member of the clergy is abusive, it is not strange for that experience to shape the way people see all clergy. This fact is supported further by the behavior of bishops who sought to cover up the abuse. As we pointed out in the second chapter, the hierarchy was more concerned with protecting the reputation of the clergy than protecting the dignity of the laity. The power of an ordained minister is a gift given through the laity. When the clergy cease to be trusted, they can no longer fulfill their role in a fruitful manner. The meaning that they are meant to convey is violated. For so many Catholics, who have been raised to make sense of the world through the lens of the Catholic sacramental worldview, when the clergy lose their meaning the meaning of the whole world falters, leaving them feeling lost, empty, and abandoned.

The clericalist culture of death makes this consequence of moral injury possible in the first place. Clericalism idolizes clergy, especially through the celebration of a liturgy that is too often seen as a ritual mechanism whereby sacred ministers dispense salvation to the passive and deferential laity. This culture places so much emphasis on the ordained minister as the central and most necessary symbol for God that the minister largely determines how all other symbols will be interpreted. Betrayal from an abusive priest is like pulling a loose thread on a sweater; when that one string begins to unravel it brings the rest of them with it. This is certainly true of isolated incidents of CPSA, but, as we know, the Catholic sex-abuse crisis is far from a series of isolated incidents committed by a few "bad apples." Rather, systemic CPSA perpetrates betrayals on a scale that is difficult to fathom. When the conduct of priests, bishops, and popes is shown to be deeply abusive, the totality of the liturgical life of the Church can begin to feel like manipulative hypocrisy.

Since the various types of moral injuries have a broad range of impacts, moral injury can affect liturgical efficacy in many different ways. The depth of the impact can vary along with the intensity with which the injury is experienced—some may be merely bothered while others experience a fundamental shift in how they are able to participate in the liturgy. Even if one's image or impression of God remains intact, the erosion of the self that is caused by moral injury can change the way that one is able to engage in spiritual practices like liturgical worship. Pope Benedict XVI attests to this reality when he writes in a 2010 pastoral letter to the Catholics of Ireland, "I know some of you find it difficult even to enter the doors of a church after all that has occurred." Systemic CPSA transforms the experience of liturgy into one of hypocrisy. The feelings of violation and betrayal brought about by moral injury can create a sense of distance between the person affected and all of their relationships, including their relationship with God. The unstable sense of self, the erosion of personhood, leads to one calling into question the nature of every connection. It is hard to be a good friend, neighbor, or partner when you don't feel like yourself, and maintaining a relationship with God is no exception.

A person's faith and spirituality are constituted by their relationship with their sources of meaning. For many Roman Catholics the cultural artifacts that make up the liturgical life of the Church (for example, biblical narratives, ordained ministers, Sunday mass, holy days, baptisms, funerals, and so on) are the symbols that they use to construct meaning in the world. This includes a sense of what is valuable and sacred (for example, human dignity, the goodness and beauty of creation, and so on) and a sense of what is good and evil. All these aspects of the liturgical life of the Church work together to cultivate a person's relationship to self, community, and God. In other words, this culture is the authority that allows Catholics to develop the relationships that constitute their identity. Louis-Marie Chauvet points out that this liturgical culture is like a womb that forms us and gives birth to us.[42]

Pointing out that the loss of meaning is intricately linked with a loss of language, symbols, and culture, theologian Denise Starkey writes:

> Intense pain not only "destroys a person's self and world," it is also "language-destroying: as the content of one's world disintegrates, so the content of one's language disintegrates; as the self disintegrates, so that which would express and project the self is robbed of its source and subject."[43]

In the context of the liturgy, this means that all of the language and symbols that were once saturated with sacred meaning begin to corrode and hollow out, becoming instead reminders of the hypocrisy and betrayal that inflicted so much pain. In short, when experienced through the lens of moral injury, the liturgy struggles to build up a worshiper's agency. Its symbols provoke feelings of anger, grief, disillusionment, and guilt. In this way the liturgy is *deformative*. It chips away at a person's sense of self and their worldview. Their spirituality erodes, and their faith begins to falter. When one's sources of authority and safety are taken away through betrayal, it can leave a person in a state where they feel they have become a spiritual orphan. The language and symbols that have formed us are shown to be lies. Generous acts of love and care are transformed into

---

[42] Louis-Marie Chauvet, *The Sacraments: The Word of God at the Mercy of the Body*, trans. Madeleine Beaumont (Collegeville, MN: Liturgical Press, 2001), 17.

[43] A. Denise Starkey, *The Shame That Lingers: A Survivor-Centered Critique of Catholic Sin-Talk* (Lausanne, Switzerland: Peter Lang Group AG, 2009), 134.

manipulation and hypocrisy. When a person is told that God loves them and that the Church is a place they will be loved unconditionally, they begin to see themselves as a beloved child of God, and they develop a sense of right and wrong that is rooted in the dignity of humans and the goodness of all creation. However, when that message is delivered through a clericalist culture that has betrayed its own message through systemic CPSA, the message itself begins to lose its meaning and, therefore, its ability to form agents of God's love.

As we draw this section to a close, we need to make two brief points: (1) moral injury does not invalidate the liturgy; and (2) moral injury does not preclude all positive experiences of the liturgy. First, as we argued in our previous chapter, trauma and PTSD do not stop the liturgy from communicating grace to some people. The same is true of the betrayals that inflict moral injury. A liturgy that feels hypocritical and manipulative to one person, may, to the person sitting nearby, be experienced as an invitation into God's love. In more traditional theological language, we are not arguing for Donatism.[44]

Second, and related to the previous point, moral injury does not preclude all beneficial experiences of liturgy. Despite the existence of moral injury in a person, it is still possible for them to have moments where the liturgy is comforting, formative, and grace filled. Depending on the type and intensity of the injury, a person's experience of the liturgy can still include beneficial and positive feelings. Like many abusive relationships, there can be moments of beauty and enjoyment. In other words, one's relationship to the liturgy and the Church is complex. Moral injury does not result in an experience of the liturgy that is binary: either all good or all bad. Acknowledging these realities is important if we want to

---

[44] For an in-depth discussion of the Donatist controversy, see Adam D. Ployd, "The Power of Baptism: Augustine's Pro-Nicene Response to the Donatists," *Journal of Early Christian Studies* 22, no. 4 (2014): 519–40.

be true to the experiences of people who are struggling from the effects of the betrayals inflicted by systemic CPSA. When people distance themselves from abuse, the distance is rarely experienced as purely good. Instead, there is a real sense of loss that accompanies avoiding abusive situations. In the final chapter of this book, we return to a discussion of how people can process the grief that accompanies losing the good that often comes alongside the pains of abuse.

Conclusion: Losing Faith

In the end, when a person is mired in intense negative emotions, such as betrayal, anger, and a loss of self-worth, the words being spoken through the liturgy can be experienced as hollow, disingenuous, and manipulative. In these moments the liturgy becomes a flagrant act of hypocrisy that further intensifies those negative feelings. Like the hundredth apology from a repeat abuser, the liturgical symbols are slowly hollowed out, becoming a dismissive slap in the face. The liturgy is supposed to be an event in which we experience God's promise of salvific love and friendship. Because of the systemic trauma inflicted by the clericalist culture of death, the liturgy is readily recognized and experienced as an empty promise from a Church and a God who simply wants the power that comes through ownership and control of others. In this way a person's faith is slowly eroded by repeated liturgical lies. The meaning of one's very existence, too, begins to deteriorate as the relationships that once provided a sense of safety and belonging are compromised. It is no wonder that the traumas of systemic CPSA have led to isolation, despair, and suicidality in so many.

When we say that moral injury can lead to a loss of faith, we do not mean to imply that a person goes from having faith to having no faith at all. When it works at its best, the liturgy is the source and summit of the Roman Catholic faith because it provides people with the cultural frameworks that form an active Catholic identity. The narratives, values, and social structures that manifest Catholic identity are communicated through liturgical symbols. When a community habitually celebrates the liturgy, they cultivate their faith and, therefore, cultivate their identity as Catholics. So, when the myriad betrayals of systemic CPSA are inflicted on that community, the resulting moral injury begins to deteriorate the liturgy's ability to form that identity. The liturgy cannot work as an offering of God's love that provokes that community's active friendship with God. Instead of becoming more like Christ, the liturgy's hollowed-out symbols provoke a sense of pain and betrayal that further isolates worshipers from themselves, from one another, and from God.

St. Augustine of Hippo wrote that, in celebrating the Eucharist, Christians behold what they are (that is, the body of Christ) so that they may more fully become what they receive.[45] Ideally, the Eucharist is God's gift of participation in the divine life of Christ. Yet the shadows of trauma that inflict moral injury can hinder the liturgy's ability to offer the Eucharist as that gift of love. Hence, when individuals lose trust in the Church and begin avoiding the liturgy, they are losing the faith they once held. As we will see in a later chapter, this does not mean they have lost all faith, nor does it mean that their salvation is called into question. The answer to the problems that we have described in this chapter is not simply healing the person, although that should be a goal. The problem does not lie in the person afflicted with moral injury. Rather, the clericalist culture of abuse is the problem. It perpetrates the betrayals of systemic CPSA, inflicting moral injury and compromising the source and summit of the Catholic faith—the liturgy.

---

[45] Augustine of Hippo, Sermon 227.

5

Losing Hope

Moral Distress and the Liturgy

> *[When they learn that their child has been abused] a parent loses their ability to be a good parent. . . . They don't want to believe that this could happen. . . . They don't want to believe that someone they trusted could hurt their child like this. . . . Because once they know, it falls on them, too. They become responsible, and for some people that's too much to handle.*
>
> —Haven Evans[1]

The celebration of the Eucharist is the most important ritual in the liturgical life of the Church. Every activity of the Church, including the rest of its liturgical life, springs from and flows toward the celebration of the Eucharist. As such, it is the source and summit of the Catholic faith. Roman Catholic sacramental theology often emphasizes this importance by highlighting the ways that Christ is truly present to the Church

---

[1] In Sam Ruland, "When Boy Told of Sexual Abuse, His Parents Asked the Priest Who Raped Him to Counsel Him," *York Daily Record* online, September 4, 2018.

when the Eucharist is celebrated. As we explained in the first chapter, the liturgical life of the Church is meant to provide an encounter with Jesus so that the Church might better conform itself to the life of love and justice that Jesus lived. So, while Jesus's presence in the Eucharist is a miraculous and gratuitous gift, his presence is not an end in itself. Rather, it is a gift that should be received as a task to be embraced and fulfilled.[2] This is why the celebration of the Eucharist is often called the mass.

In the Latin version of the Roman Rite (that is, the Roman Catholic version of the Eucharist), the presider concludes the celebration of the Eucharist with the phrase *Ite, missa est*." In English, this phrase is usually translated as, "Go, the mass has ended." However, a more literal translation would be, "Go, it is dismissed." The Latin word *missa* means "to be sent, dismissed, or released." This is where the English word *mission* comes from. To be sent on a mission means that a person or community has a task to be accomplished. In other words, just as Jesus sent his disciples out into the world, the ordained minister ends the celebration of the Eucharist by sending the congregation out into the world to preach the good news by the way they live their lives in service to justice. Hence, the word *mass* literally means "to be sent on a mission." In fact, the most recent versions of the Roman Missal provide other options for the closing lines of the mass that are intended to better emphasize the fact that the congregation is being sent on a mission. For example, the deacon, or, in his absence, the priest, might choose to say, "Go in peace, glorifying the Lord by your life."[3] In short, the Eucharist is intended to be spiritual food that nourishes the Church, conforming it to Christ,

---

[2] Louis-Marie Chauvet, *The Sacraments: The Word of God at the Mercy of the Body*, trans. Madeleine Beaumont (Collegeville, MN: Liturgical Press, 2001), 65.

[3] United States Conference of Catholic Bishops, Roman Missal.

so that it might leave the mass, go into the world, and be the presence of Christ's love for everyone they meet.

Why do we begin a chapter that will examine the relationship between moral distress and the liturgy with a reflection on the etymology of the term *mass*? In short, we want to emphasize the fact that the purpose of the mass (and, therefore, the entire liturgical life of the Church) is to form a community of people who are capable and ready to use their agency to live active lives of faith, hope, and love. This means that the Roman Catholic community is called and sent to work for peace and justice in the world. As we have seen in the previous chapters, trauma can damage the liturgy's ability to form agents who are capable and ready to live this way. Post-traumatic stress disorder (PTSD) can transform the liturgy into an experience of violence that does immense damage to a person's agency, and moral injury can damage the trust and faith that are necessary for a person to grow as a disciple of Christ. Having explored the ways PTSD and moral injury can affect the fruitfulness of the liturgy, we turn now to another common consequence of the Roman Catholic sexual-abuse crisis: moral distress.

Primarily manifested by a sense of guilt and powerlessness when experiencing or witnessing an abusive act, moral distress usually accompanies (or is understood to be part of) PTSD and moral injury. In essence, a person experiencing moral distress is suffering from a sense of being complicit in an abusive system that is causing harm, while simultaneously feeling powerless to act otherwise. This awareness does not need to be accurate; what matters is the *perception* that one is participating in a harmful act, either by action or inaction. For example, when a Catholic becomes aware of the depth and breadth of systemic CPSA (clergy perpetrated sexual abuse), moral distress can arise as they reflect on their role in maintaining and perpetuating a clericalist culture of death. A good priest who has never personally abused anyone may rightly begin to feel responsible for the sex-abuse crisis as they reflect on the way they have presided over liturgies that form people who value self-sacrifice and docility. Similarly, a lay person who has never been aware of any abuse happening in their parish might nevertheless begin to feel complicit in the sex-abuse crisis as they reflect on the way their liturgical worship has cultivated clericalist ministers. As this awareness builds, a sense of distress can begin to arise.

While the old phrase "no snowflake in an avalanche ever feels responsible" can be true, it is by no means always accurate. Many people develop a keen awareness of contributing to abusive cultures despite their desires and efforts to live lives of peace and justice. The same is certainly true for many Catholics who become aware of the enormity of the sex-abuse crisis. This chapter begins by examining the nature of moral distress, seeking to show how a sense of complicity and powerlessness can deteriorate one's agency. Then we examine the way that moral distress affects the liturgical life of the Church. Our goal is to show that experiencing guilt and powerlessness can lead to a profound sense of resignation and hopelessness. When the liturgy is celebrated by people who are struggling to find hope, the goal of forming agents who are ready to work for peace and justice is greatly hindered.

What Is Moral Distress?

Like moral injury, moral distress is a concept in development. Those who study moral distress have not reached a perfect consensus on its meaning.[4] However, the vast majority of

---

[4] For a helpful and concise overview review of the way this concept has developed and of how researchers have attempted to define moral distress, its causes, and its effects, see Joan McCarthy and Chris Gastmans, "Moral

researchers see moral distress as a concept used to describe ethical dissonance between one's values and one's experiences. Moral distress is manifested by a perceived lack of agency to do what one knows is ethical in a troubling situation. It occurs when one has a strong sense of the moral thing to be done in a given situation, while being unable to follow through due to external constraints, even if those external constraints have been internalized. The term *moral distress* was coined in 1984 by philosopher and medical ethicist Andrew Jameton to describe the experiences of nurses and healthcare professionals when they are directed to act in ways that conflict with their deeply held beliefs.[5] For example, moral distress may occur when a nurse believes the right thing to do for a patient differs from an order from a physician, or when the appropriate course of treatment is painful and the nurse is uncomfortable with inflicting pain on the patient, even in service of the greater good. Moral distress is brought about by feeling powerless in the face of a difficult situation, especially when, if given a choice, one would act differently.

One of the most helpful contributions of moral distress as a concept is that it draws attention to the various and complex relationships that influence a person's moral reasoning. In other words, when experiencing moral distress, a person is in conflict with a context that is shaped by the sociopolitical, cultural, and interpersonal environment.[6] Nursing professors Edison Luiz Devos Barlem and Flávia Regina Souza Ramos argue that

> moral distress could also be defined as a painful feeling or psychological imbalance resulting from recognising an

---

Distress: A Review of the Argument-Based Nursing Ethics Literature," *Nursing Ethics* 22, no. 1 (2015): 131–52, esp. 136–41.

[5] McCarthy and Gastmans, 131–52.

[6] McCarthy and Gastmans.

ethically correct action that cannot be performed because of hindrances such as lack of time, reluctant supervisors or a power structure that may inhibit a moral, political, institutional or juridical action.[7]

Because a nurse's job involves navigating a complex system of responsibilities and expectations from an array of stakeholders who often have conflicting values, the nurse can quickly find themselves experiencing distress that arises from conflicting demands that are often mutually exclusive. For example, a good nurse should simultaneously (1) prioritize their patient's health, (2) care for five patients at once, (3) be kind and attentive to each patient and their family members, (4) not challenge the attending physician's expertise and authority, (5) defer to the charge nurse's orders, and (6) work fast enough to make their employer a profit, (7) all while caring for themselves so they can avoid burning out. This is an overly simplified and incomplete list of what many nurses experience during every shift. Unsurprisingly, a common result of being consistently exposed to moral distress is burnout and resignation from one's job.[8] In essence, moral distress is experienced as a slow erasure of one's agency. In both overt and covert ways, external pressures slowly take a person's voice away, teaching them that it is better to remain quiet and passive than to try repeatedly to fight against the status quo.

Traditionally, the restraints that lead to moral distress were related to employment. Moral distress has typically been tied to the nursing profession, but it is evident that it can be felt any-

---

[7] Edison Luiz Devos Barlem and Flávia Regina Souza Ramos, "Constructing a Theoretical Model of Moral Distress," *Nursing Ethics* 22, no. 5 (2015): 608–15.

[8] Vidette Todaro-Franceschi, *Compassion Fatigue and Burnout in Nursing: Enhancing Professional Quality of Life*, second ed. (Cham, Switzerland: Springer Publishing Company, 2019), 101.

time an individual cannot act in accordance with their moral code due to feelings of powerlessness. Social authority, age, race, ability, gender, or other socially constructed power dynamics have the potential to bring about a morally distressing situation. Many professions involve situations that foster moral distress, as do many other forms of social groups, including religious communities. Given the hierarchical organizational structure of the Catholic Church, both laity and clergy are consistently in contexts that might provoke moral distress. Both positions require submission to an authority where beliefs and values may not always feel aligned.

Someone can unwillingly participate in an immoral action due to a lack of knowledge of how to navigate the situation, like not knowing who to report something to, or who to go to for help, or when rules and regulations might restrict action. Fear of retaliation or losing community and social support could also be influential factors. Paradoxically, the distress that occurs in these situations is a feeling of guilt for committing or contributing to an action that is ultimately outside one's control. This differs from a more common sense of guilt, where the sense of remorse and responsibility ideally leads to a commitment to change one's behavior in the future. With moral distress, the sense of powerlessness that accompanies the guilt creates a situation where one cannot course correct or do anything different should a similar situation arise again; there is a helplessness and hopelessness associated with the situation, which is the key element that triggers moral distress.[9]

From this description of moral distress as an experience of powerlessness leading to a sense of resignation, it is easy to see that most traumatic events that lead to PTSD often result in acute forms of moral distress. When a person is abused or

---

[9] Barlem and Ramos, "Constructing a Theoretical Model of Moral Distress," 608–15.

assaulted, shame, self-blame, and a feeling of helplessness are often experienced during and in the aftermath of the event. In addition to this close connection to PTSD, moral distress has significant overlaps with moral injury and has many similarities. For instance, moral injury can be experienced by a person who committed a harmful act against another person. As such, moral injury can also involve a sense of guilt and shame. However, moral distress differs from moral injury primarily in its emphasis on a person's sense of guilt accompanied by a feeling of powerlessness and resignation. It creates a sense of complicity in the actor, because they feel that they should have acted differently, even though the cost of behaving in alignment with their values was too significant to do so. While moral injury is primarily a loss of trust that results from exposure to betrayal, moral distress is generally understood to be a result of participating in a morally troubling event and feeling powerless to opt out. With moral distress, there is a greater sense of personal responsibility and moral failure because a person is pressured into acting contrary to their conscience. In short, the difference between moral distress and moral injury is the experience of having done something immoral instead of having had something immoral happen to you.

Moral Distress and Clericalist Culture

Given this description of moral distress, we turn now to examine the causes and effects of moral distress in the context of systemic CPSA. The existing research on moral distress in healthcare settings describes the "moral residue" left upon individuals who are affected by consistent moral distress. According to nursing professors Adam T. Booth and Becky J. Christian: "Moral residue is the lingering experience created from unresolved morally distressing events, which pile-up and lead to further distress. Moral residue may crescendo and become unmanageable, manifesting as conscientious objection, emotional and psychological distancing from the ethical dimensions of practice, burnout, and/or withdrawal [from work]."[10] In other words, feelings of guilt, anger, frustration, and hopelessness build up and have a compounding effect when a person repeatedly feels powerless to avoid participation in an immoral system. These residual effects of moral distress affect more than the psychological dimension of the person who is suffering moral distress. Individuals who are afflicted with moral distress have reported biological symptoms as well, including heart palpitations, diarrhea, and headaches. As with PTSD and moral injury, the harmful effects of moral distress influence an individual's physical, mental, social, and spiritual health.

If we imagine an individual's moral commitments as armor, allowing them to protect their conscience and maintain agency, consistent exposure to moral distress chips away at this armor. Feelings of worthlessness, a lack of agency, and chronic powerlessness compound, waging a war against a person's armor. If this assault is maintained, the armor becomes ineffective, ultimately leading to compromised moral sensitivity (that is, compassion fatigue) and resignation. For example, if an individual is exposed to situations where they feel powerless at work, they may stop asserting themselves outside of work as well, as their armor is chipped down by repeated moral distress. The resulting passivity can lead to desensitization and demoralization.

So, how do moral distress and the moral residue it creates relate to the sex-abuse crisis? Given our description of

---

[10] Adam T. Booth and Becky J. Christian, "Surgical Intensive Care Unit Nurses' Coping With Moral Distress and Moral Residue: A Descriptive Qualitative Approach," *Dimensions of Critical Care Nursing* 43, no. 6 (2024): 298-99.

clericalism in the second chapter, it should be readily apparent that the pervasiveness of clericalism in the Catholic Church makes moral distress a common experience for many Catholics. The clericalist culture of death that serves as the foundation for the sex-abuse crisis is marked by a deeply hierarchical organization, in which authority and power are reserved for ordained ministers (especially the bishops), and the laity are largely relegated to a position of deference. In the Catholic Church, ordained ministers control the culture, including the liturgical life of the Church. Hence, the feeling of powerlessness is common when a Catholic is confronted with awareness of clericalism and its role in causing systemic CPSA. In the context of clericalism, there are many reasons why a Catholic might feel complicit and hindered from being able to act in a moral way. On an individual and personal level, a lay person may feel unable to question or challenge a priest's harmful behaviors. When Catholics are taught to see ordained ministers as representatives of God, challenging their authority is tantamount to blasphemy. Much like the biblical figure Job, Catholics who question the abusive behavior of a priest or a bishop can be left feeling that their voice is meaningless because they are so inferior to the sacred minister. Better that they simply accept the abuse and repent in dust and ashes.

On a more macro level, Catholics can feel a sense of powerlessness due to being marginalized from any decision-making structures. For example, one way that the Roman Catholic Church often maintains clerical authority is by describing tradition (that is, doctrines, scripture interpretations, liturgical rubrics, and so forth) as a set of revealed and unchanging truths. Even when a teaching has gone through a clear, substantial change (for example, the doctrine of salvation outside the Church, the matter of the ordination rite, and so on), that change is framed as a development or evolution that assures the unbroken credibility of the magisterium's authority. The teachings and practices of the Church are presented by some Catholic leaders as though they are not up for debate. When bishops do decide to open up controversial issues for discussion, laity are invited to participate in structured ways that are quickly reduced to advisory roles. For example, in recent years Pope Francis rightly emphasized a need for a more synodal approach to discerning reforms in the Church. The synodal process is intended to be an opportunity for the hierarchy to listen deeply to the experiences and concerns of the laity. Yet, like many political townhall listening sessions, the synodal process can function like an empty ritual meant to placate people by making them feel listened to. Even more saddening, some bishops simply eschewed participation in the process, clearly showing their lack of interest in hearing the laity's concerns and insights altogether. In the end, the results leave many in the Church feeling dismissed and powerless.[11]

These are but two brief examples of how clericalism fosters moral distress. Some Catholics who want to participate meaningfully in guiding the life of the Church are left with a sense of having no choice but to fall back in line and play within the rules. As these experiences of erasure multiply over a lifetime of trying to be faithful to the Church, the guilt, frustration, and anger begin to compound in what nursing professors Elizabeth Gingell Epstein and Ann Baile Hamric call the crescendo effect.[12] Each subsequent experience of moral distress is felt more acutely. With each new report of sexual abuse

---

[11] Thomas Reese, "Synod Ends with Disappointment and Hope," *National Catholic Reporter* online, November 7, 2024; Jonathan Leidl, "As Synod's End Nears, Progressives Brace for Disappointment—and Blame Organizers," *National Catholic Register* online, October 23, 2024; John L. Allen, Jr., "Disappointment in All Directions: Is Anyone Actually Happy with the Outcome of the Synod on Synodality?" *Catholic Herald* online, November 16, 2024.

[12] Elizabeth Gingell Epstein and Ann Baile Hamric, "Moral Distress, Moral Residue, and the Crescendo Effect," *The Journal of Clinical Ethics* 20, no. 4 (2009): 330–42.

and each new revelation of another bishop who has failed to report abuse or sought to cover it up, the moral distress grows in intensity. In the end, one can be left with the feeling that the only moral thing to do is to walk away from the situation, and many Catholics have done just that. Yet, walking away from one's native culture, which provides the basis for one's most intimate relationships and one's foundational values, is no simple or easy task. When a person believes that disaffiliation is the right thing to do but simply cannot bring themselves to do it, hopelessness and resignation can arise.

When practicing Catholics who have not directly experienced sexual abuse become aware of the depth and breadth of the sexual-abuse crisis, their initial reaction might be more akin to moral injury. A sense of betrayal can arise, leading to diminishing trust that can go so far as to constitute a crisis of faith. However, beyond this sense of moral injury, they can begin to reflect on their role in the Church's culture and develop a sense of complicity in the Church's abusive culture. When the global extent of the cover-up is recognized, it becomes nearly impossible to overlook the cultural roots of the problem. In other words, the sex-abuse crisis is recognized as a logical consequence of the clericalist culture of death.

There are situations where cooperation in wrongdoing is inevitable, but the doctrine of complicity aims to explore the limits of cooperation in a given context.[13] Some potential types of involvement are: formal cooperation (helping someone do what is wrong knowingly in a way that endorses the behavior, like driving the getaway car for a robber), immediate material cooperation (where you don't necessarily approve, but take an active part in the wrongdoing for some benefit, like selling someone a weapon who you know has a history of violent acts), and mediate material cooperation (where the action or

---

[13] Stephen R. Latham, "Moral Distress and Cooperation with Wrongdoing," *American Journal of Bioethics* 16, no. 12 (2016): 31–32.

benefit isn't necessary for the wrongful act but could support it indirectly, like banking at an institution that heavily invests in oil or working as a custodian in an office of a politician you find morally objectionable). The doctrine of complicity permits mediate material cooperation depending on the proximity of the wrongdoing, the reason for participating, and the way it might influence others to act in the future. The doctrine of complicity ties back to clerical culture, in which hierarchical structures create a complex moral landscape for both clergy and laity. Clericalism often fosters an environment in which members of the Church, both inside and outside the hierarchy, may feel morally constrained from speaking out or taking action against such a crisis. This dynamic makes it challenging to separate individual participation in liturgy from the broader institutional failings that contribute to the CPSA crisis. Clericalism generates a sense of powerlessness and a lack of trust that mirror the conditions that give rise to mediate material cooperation, where individuals may feel complicit by association despite not directly supporting the wrongdoing. In this way clericalist culture amplifies the moral distress that laity experience, as lay participation in liturgical rituals feels inextricably linked to a system that is riddled with failures to address serious moral wrongs.

Moral Distress Hindering Liturgical Efficacy

How, then, do feelings of guilt, resignation, and hopelessness impact the fruitfulness of the liturgy? First, moral distress can hinder liturgical efficacy if worshipers' moral residue essentially erases their motivation to work for peace and justice. Through learning about the breadth and depth of the sex-abuse crisis and futilely attempting to enact change, they can lose hope to such an extent that they are no longer motivated to respond to the provocative invitation of the liturgy. If anyone, clergy or laity, celebrates the liturgy with a disposition of apathy and resignation, the liturgical symbols will not be internalized and used as motivation to live as Christ in the world. When moral agents feel powerless, they reduce their engagement, disconnecting from their ability to participate, even if they might want to.

Second, as we discussed in the first chapter, clericalist culture is cultivated by a liturgy that seeks passivity and docility. While the Second Vatican Council enacted reforms that were intended to create liturgical celebrations with full, active participation as the goal, this goal is not always realized. Unfortunately, some liturgical celebrations still treat members of the congregation as though they are passive sheep whose primary value is to build up the power and authority of the clergy. In this way the liturgy is a practice of passivity. The practice of passivity makes the descent into moral resignation easier. Hence, the liturgy ceases to build up the worshipers' agency. The guilt and hopelessness that emerge through an awareness of clericalism and the sex-abuse crisis are exacerbated by a liturgy that instills passivity. Moral distress, then, leads to resignation, as a person may feel that they cannot act morally, so it would be better to not act at all. Shaped by liturgies that value passivity, the person can escape into a worldview where their agency plays no role. This world is built by a liturgy that requires no participation, preferring docile sheep whose existence only serves the shepherds. Moral distress can make someone search for an escape. Resignation can push a person more deeply into a liturgy that lacks participation. Passively attending a liturgy that dispenses a commodified grace absolves a person from the responsibility to cooperate with grace. Instead of striving to become more like Jesus in their daily lives, the laity are satisfied with avoiding hell by making sure they fulfill their liturgical obligations. Of course, if you orient your life on earth to only avoid going to hell after you die, it can be easy to overlook your mission to create heaven on earth. Ironically, then, attempting to avoid hell after death ends up creating hell on earth. In this way hopelessness begets hopelessness.

Third, and perhaps more problematic for the liturgical life of the Church, moral distress can hinder liturgical efficacy when a Catholic begins to see the liturgy itself as a participation in the Church's clericalist culture of death. When this happens, a worshiper believes that, simply by entering a Church and participating in the liturgy, their actions are contributing, however minimally, to the cultivation of clericalist ministers. By piously following the rhythms of the mass, by patiently listening to the sermon, by lining up to be hand-fed the Eucharist, and by all the other liturgical actions that perform, manifest, and perpetuate the laity's inferiority to the clergy, participating in the liturgy renders a person complicit in the culture that sexually abuses people and then protects the abusers. If the sexual-abuse crisis is fundamentally about clerics maintaining power, then participating in liturgies that place those clerics in a position of power cannot be a purely innocent activity. In this way moral distress drives people away from the liturgy. When they cannot participate without feeling like they are betraying themselves and others, they feel as though they must distance or leave in order to maintain a clear conscience.

In all of these cases the fruitfulness of the liturgy is compromised. On one hand, if, due to an overwhelming sense of guilt, the worshiper decides to avoid liturgical celebrations, the liturgy cannot work for them as it is intended. On the other hand, if, due to a sense of hopelessness and resignation, the worshiper continues attending mass with a passive, detached disposition, the liturgy cannot work as intended. Either way, the disposition necessary for the liturgy to bear fruit in the lives of the worshiper is compromised. Someone who is severely affected by moral distress and has developed a sense of complicity and/or resignation will not be able to hear the exhortation at the conclusion of mass as a provocative invitation: "Go in peace, glorifying the Lord by your life." Hopelessness can steal away the self-worth that allows a person to live a life of love and justice.

So, in the wake of moral distress, liturgical rituals can cease to be primarily provocative signs of God's love and are, rather, experienced as participation in systemic sexual assault. As with moral injury, moral distress hinders liturgical efficacy because it undoes the predisposition that is necessary to experience the liturgy as the offering of grace. If, as we said above, the liturgy is intended to provoke a grace-filled way of living, then moral distress confounds that intention and instills a sense of helplessness and resignation.[14]

Conclusion: Church-Perpetuated Sexual Abuse

To conclude this chapter, we return to the difference between moral injury and moral distress and the effects they have on the liturgy. Moral injury can make the liturgy feel like hypocritical manipulation. After experiencing the myriad betrayals of the sex-abuse crisis, a worshiper is left with shaken *faith*. Moral injury, then, comes from an awareness of systemic CPSA. Moral distress can make the liturgy feel like an immoral activity. When one develops a sense of complicity that leads to resignation, the worshiper is left with shaken *hope*. Moral distress, then, comes from an awareness of the ways that the Church perpetuates sexual abuse.

While systemic CPSA is undoubtedly the fault of the direct abuser and the bishops who protect him, we can also say that those who participate in a clericalist culture have contributed

---

[14] David Farina Turnbloom, Megan Breen, Noah Lamberger, and Kate Seddon, "Liturgy in the Shadow of Trauma," *Religions* 13, no. 7 (2022): 583.

to perpetuating systemic CPSA. In other words, the Catholic sex-abuse crisis is clergy-perpetrated sexual abuse *and* Church-perpetuated sexual abuse. To be clear, we are *not* saying that everyone in the Catholic Church is morally responsible for systemic CPSA, and we are *not* saying that everyone who is responsible is equally responsible. Rather, we are saying that, much like a tax-paying American who grapples with the reality that their taxes are used to fund immoral activity (for example, environmental degradation, militaristic colonialism, and so on), a Catholic can rightly arrive at a sense of being complicit in the clericalism that has fostered the abuse of countless innocent victims.

The question, then, is how does one respond to this awareness? As we have pointed out, moral distress can make cultural change feel impossible. It can be tempting to resign oneself and escape into a worldview that focuses on salvation in an afterlife. This option will, of course, simply promise more of the same abuse. Alternatively, it can feel easier to focus on healing those who have been harmed by systemic CPSA. This option is a vital one that demands attention and continual effort. Yet we know that no lasting healing can occur if we do not acknowledge and address the causes of the abuse. We must be willing to treat the entire disease and not solely the symptoms. The next part of this book suggests ways that the Church might work toward the cultural reform that is necessary if further abuse is going to cease and if deep and lasting healing is going to occur.

6

Toward a Relational Ordained Ministry

We put them on pedestals, almost to the point where I thought they were superhuman in a sense. . . . When he tried to tell and went to the police, he was laughed off.[1]
—David Nolan

Throughout the preceding three chapters we have explored the symptoms of trauma that impair the efficacy of the liturgy. In these final three chapters, we turn our attention to how one might reform the clericalist culture that has cultivated and inflicted the sexual-abuse crisis on the Church, heavily impeding the liturgy that is meant to sustain and culminate its life. In the wake of the sexual-abuse crisis much has been written about clericalism and the ways the Church might carry out the desperately needed work of reform.[2] We limit our focus to issues

---

[1] In Ashamed M. Muhammad, "Catholic Church Accused of Denying Justice to Blacks Abused by Priests," *The Final Call* online, December 8, 2009.

[2] Gerald A. Arbuckle, *Abuse and Cover-up: Refounding the Catholic Church in Trauma* (Maryknoll, NY: Orbis Books, 2019); George B. Wilson, *Clericalism: The Death of Priesthood* (Collegeville, MN: Liturgical Press, 2008); Susan K. Wood and Michael Downey, *Ordering the Baptismal Priesthood: Theologies of Lay and Ordained Ministry* (Collegeville, MN: Liturgical Press, 2003).

that are directly related to the celebration of the liturgy. Our examinations of post-traumatic stress disorder (PTSD), moral injury, and moral distress all addressed the impact that clericalist culture has had on liturgical efficacy through the ongoing tragedy of the sexual-abuse crisis. The traumas inflicted by the clericalist culture have (1) turned the liturgy into an experience of dehumanizing violence for those suffering from PTSD, (2) turned the liturgy into an act of hypocrisy and betrayal for those suffering from moral injury, and (3) turned the liturgy into a participation in systemic abuse for those suffering from moral distress. As we have seen, the sex-abuse crisis has cast these shadows of trauma over the liturgy and greatly affect the liturgy's ability to fruitfully offer salvation to the Church. So, while it is important to focus attention on healing these harmful symptoms of trauma, it is equally important to treat the cultural disease causing these symptoms to ensure that this abuse does not continue.

In the present chapter we examine the way that the Church's theologies of ordained ministry influence how priests and bishops behave and how they are understood and treated by the laity. Specifically, we focus on the difference between seeing ordained ministry through the lenses of substance ontology and relational ontology. Substance ontology encourages a way of seeing priests and bishops as members of a sacred and superior caste who serve as gatekeepers of God's salvific grace. Relational ontology, in contrast, sees the authority and liturgical role of ministers as something that is given as a gift through their relationship to the laity.

When the harms caused by the sex-abuse crisis are fully appreciated, we cannot ignore the fact that the liturgical life of the Church has been shaken to its foundations. As we have seen, stubbornly insisting on the liturgy's invincibility is not a sign of piety; it is a sign of clericalism and the Church's self-idolatry. As the liturgy itself teaches, one must begin with honestly confessing their sins if there is to be any hope of transformation. So, let us turn now to an examination of the dangerous ways the Church has understood and treated its ordained ministers.

Ordained Ministry Rooted in Substance Ontology

As we discussed in the second chapter, Pope Francis referred to clericalism as a culture of death that "arises from an elitist and exclusivist vision of vocation, that interprets the ministry received as a *power* to be exercised rather than as a free and generous service to be given."[3] Here, we examine the way ordained ministry is often framed by the Church as an elite caste with exclusive powers. To this end, let us begin by unpacking the phrase *substance ontology*.

Simply stated, the word *ontology* refers to something's existence. The characteristics, properties, and relationships that define something constitute its ontology. The word *substance,* on the other hand, is used to refer to those aspects of something's being that exist independently of its relationships. Therefore, a substance ontology is a way of understanding something that focuses on the capabilities and characteristics that exist independently of its contexts. So, when we use the phrase *substance ontology* to describe ordained ministers, we are emphasizing a way of understanding priests' identity that prioritizes their power and characteristics as though they were something independent of the minister's relationships. When described through the lens of substance ontology, we might describe an ordained minister

---

[3] Pope Francis, "Address by His Holiness Pope Francis at the Opening of the Synod of Bishops on Young People, the Faith and Vocational Discernment," October 2018.

as a man who has the power to govern the Church, preach, absolve sins, and consecrate the Eucharist. In Pope Francis's words, clericalism is described as a power to be exercised.

To illustrate the dangers of overemphasizing the substance ontology of ordained ministry, consider the dangers of money. There are people who idolize wealth. They rightfully see their wealth as a form of power, but instead of loving the good they can accomplish with their power, they love the way they are *perceived as powerful*. So, instead of using the wealth for good, they hoard it so that people will continue to see them as powerful. When this happens, being seen as good is only useful insofar as it helps maintain wealth and power. They lose sight of the fact that wealth is a gift to be used for the good of all and not a self-serving commodity they have rightfully earned.[4] This idolatry of wealth is analogous to what it means to let a sacramental character become an idolized power.

In Roman Catholic sacramental theology, the substance ontology of ordained ministry is emphasized by references to something called an "indelible spiritual character."[5] When explaining the different spiritual characters that are caused by the sacraments of baptism, confirmation, and holy orders, Thomas Aquinas compares them to the permanent tattoos that soldiers would receive when they enlisted in the

---

[4] The liturgy of the Eucharist attests to this fact when it emphasizes that the gifts we offer to God are indeed "the work of human hands," yet, more fundamentally, "through God's goodness we have received the gifts we offer." The entire tradition of ritual sacrifice exists to remind humans that everything we own is a gratuitous gift from God, including our ability to work and "earn" anything. As such, our wealth and property is not simply ours to do with as we see fit. Our wealth is a gift that is given to us for a purpose: so that, as a community, we might all flourish and more fully participate in the divine life of God.

[5] *Catechism of the Catholic Church, Second Edition, Revised in Accordance with the Official Latin Text Promulgated by Pope John Paul II* (Vatican City: Libreria Editrice Vaticana, 1997), #1581–84.

military.[6] These tattoos marked them as set apart for a particular purpose. Put differently, these indelible characters deputed these soldiers for a specific mission. Their tattoos were permanent signs of their new identity as soldiers, an identity that pointed to their unique capabilities to carry out their duty as members of the military. Similarly, for Aquinas, the sacrament of holy orders leaves a permanent spiritual character on the soul of the person being ordained. The permanence of this change is signified by the use of sacred chrism to anoint the person being ordained. Sacred chrism is a perfumed oil that is difficult to wash off and gives the anointed person a sweet aroma. As such, the sacred chrism is an outward sign of the internal and indelible change that has occurred. The ordained person is permanently changed into someone who has been set apart (that is, consecrated) for serving the Church as a priest or bishop. Further, Aquinas emphasizes that this indelible character should be understood as a power (that is, a potency or capacity) that is unique to those who are ordained. As Vatican II recognized in its summary document on priests in the early church, this power allows them to preach, to celebrate the sacraments, and to govern the Church. Hence, Roman Catholic theologians often use the language "ontological change" to refer to the change that a person undergoes when being ordained to the priesthood. In short, the theology of ordained ministry that focuses its attention on the conferral of this unique power emphasizes a substance ontology.

Roman Catholic theologian Richard Gaillardetz describes this way of understanding ordained ministers:

> This shift in the understanding of ordination and ordained ministry in the second millennium was metaphysically underwritten by a substance ontology that

---

[6] Thomas Aquinas, *Summa Theologiae*, III, Q. 63, A. 1, co.

> attended primarily to those changes effected in a particular individual. This made it possible to identify ordained ministry in terms of the unique powers that were conferred through ordination. Many Western treatments of sacramental character have succumbed to the limitations of such a substance ontology, namely, that it makes ontological claims regarding the individual abstracted from his or her relational existence within the life of the church.[7]

Gaillardetz's point here is that an overly narrow focus on substance ontology eschews consideration of the particular relationships that greatly influence and define an ordained minister's identity and mission. Instead, the emphasis is placed on the "powers that were conferred through ordination." To better illustrate this way of understanding ordained ministry, briefly consider the liturgical ritual that confers the indelible character to Catholic priests and bishops: the rites of ordination.

In the Roman Catholic Church, an order is a group of people who serve the life of the Church in a distinct manner. For example, there are three ministerial orders. Deacons are members of an order known as the diaconate, which comes from the Greek word for "servant." Similarly, presbyters (the ministers usually referred to as priests) are members of the presbyterate, which comes from the Greek word for "elder." Finally, bishops are members of an order known as the episcopate, which comes from the Greek word for "overseer."[8] People are initiated into these ministerial orders by a type of ritual known as the sacrament of holy orders. Another common term for these rituals is an *ordination*. Throughout the his-

---

[7] Richard R. Gaillardetz, "Towards a Contemporary Theology of the Diaconate," *Worship* 79, no. 5 (2005): 426.

[8] It is worth noting that all of these titles describe a responsibility to the community (that is, a relational identity).

tory of the Church, ordination rituals have been done in many different ways.[9] However, among the most consistent ritual practices during ordinations are (1) the imposition of hands by a bishop, which is accompanied by a prayer of consecration, and (2) a ceremony known as the *traditio instrumentorum,* during which the person being ordained is given the "instruments" that are proper to the duties of that order. For example, during an ordination to the presbyterate, the newly consecrated priest receives a paten and chalice, instruments that are central to the celebration of the Eucharist. Receiving them during the ordination is meant to emphasize the purpose of the ordination: service to the sacramental life of the Church.

From the early Scholastic period (that is, 1100 CE) and up to the twentieth century, the *traditio instrumentorum* was explicitly named as the essential part of the ritual that accomplished the creation of a priest, initiating him into ordained ministry. These instruments were understood to be the essential matter of the sacrament because the purpose of being a priest (that is, the most essential aspect of his identity) was his relationship of service to the laity, which was primarily accomplished by leading the liturgical life of the Church. However, this emphasis on the ordained minister's relationship to the laity was fundamentally changed in the twentieth century. In his 1947 apostolic constitution *Sacramentum Ordinis,* Pope Pius XII changed the Church's teaching and asserted that the essential "matter" of holy orders is *solely* the imposition of the bishop's hands during the consecration, with this act alone being necessary to confer ordination (SO, 4).[10] By denying the

---

[9] For more in-depth examinations of the theology and history of ordination rituals, see Paul F. Bradshaw, *Rites of Ordination: Their History and Theology* (Collegeville, MN: Liturgical Press, 2013); Susan K. Wood, *Sacramental Orders* (Collegeville, MN: Liturgical Press, 2000).

[10] *Catechism of the Catholic Church,* #1573; Adam DeVille, "The Sacrament of Orders Dogmatically Understood," in *The Oxford Handbook of Sacramental*

necessity of the *traditio instrumentorum* for the validity of the ordination, the focus of the ritual becomes the consecration as the moment when power (that is, the indelible character) is conferred through one ordained minister to another. Put simply, emphasizing consecration means emphasizing ordained ministers as the exclusive source of grace. Substance ontology eschews consideration of the *purpose* of the minister and, therefore, the *purpose* of the liturgy. By denying the importance of the instruments, ordained ministers are set further apart from laity, reaffirming the clergy's status as a self-sufficient, elite caste whose power comes immediately from God (that is, without need for mediation through or cooperation with the laity).

Pope John Paul II took this emphasis further when, through the work of the Congregation for the Clergy, he published the document *The Priest, Pastor, and Minister of the Parish Community* (*PPM*). In this instructional document, the Church explicitly denies that the authority and power of the ordained minister in any way relies on their relationship to the laity:

> The function of guiding the community as shepherd, the proper function of the parish priest, stems from his unique relation to Christ the Head and Shepherd. It is a function having a sacramental character. *It is not entrusted to the priest by the community, but, through the Bishop*, it comes to him from the Lord. (*PPM*, #5)

The priest's identity is defined by the authority and power he has been given solely through the bishops; the laity are not instruments used by God to grant authority. That role is reserved exclusively for the bishops. In other words, the hierarchical structure of the Church is a top-down system of power,

---

Theology, ed. Hans Boersma and Matthew Levering (Oxford, UK: Oxford University Press, 2015), 534.

with the laity occupying a largely passive and auxiliary role. Emphasizing a substance ontology, then, allows the Church to understand ordained ministers as members of an elite caste who interpret their ministry as a power that they have inherited from the "top" and that is to be exercised "downward." This entails seeing the laity as an inferior caste with less dignity; they are seen and treated as powerless sheep who exist for the fulfillment of the shepherds.

Of course, ordination rituals are by no means the only liturgies where we can see traces of a preoccupation with the ordained minister's unique powers and elite status. Whenever sacramental theology or a liturgical celebration fetishizes the ordained minister by hyperbolically magnifying the contrast between the laity and the ordained (for example, overly ornate vestments, ordained ministers eating the entire broken hosts before the congregation receives communion, asking lay persons to kneel in front of ministers to receive the Eucharist on their tongue, and so forth), the liturgy contributes to fostering clerics marked by clericalism.[11] Of course, none of these actions are directly or uniquely responsible for the sexual-abuse crisis. Yet, they all compound to nurture a clericalist culture of abuse by reinforcing the difference between abuser and abused as a difference of substance rather than a malformed relationship. Hence, as we pointed out in the fifth chapter, the liturgical life of the Church can be an activity that cultivates a clericalist culture, resulting in an awareness of being complicit in the abuse. By ritually emphasizing the substance ontology of the ordained minister, liturgies can contribute to the abusive culture of clericalism that has fostered the sexual-abuse crisis.

---

[11] To be clear, these liturgical actions are not necessarily *intended* to cultivate a clericalist culture. They may have other beneficial meanings. However, insofar as they exacerbate the elite status of the clergy, they are actions that participate in and foster clericalist culture.

The substance ontology at the heart of a clericalist theology of ordination becomes a framework for creating an elite caste of Christians that is more valuable than the laity. The Church's Code of Canon Law, for example, points out that disrespect to clergy is more grievous than disrespect of lay people. Any assault on the pope results in an automatic excommunication (that is, *latae sententiae* excommunication), and any assault on a bishop results in automatic exclusion from the liturgical life of the Church (that is, *latae sententiae* interdict).[12] In other words, the members of the episcopate are so elevated above the laity in dignity that an assault on them is instantly unbecoming of one's communion with the Christ. Compare these codified punishments to how the Church has treated ordained ministers who sexually assault someone. The silencing of clergy perpetrated sexual abuse (CPSA) victims and the protective relocation of abusive clerics is quite different from automatic excommunication. Or, perhaps even more egregious, a high-ranking prelate like Bernard Cardinal Law, the archbishop of Boston at the time that the reports of the sex-abuse crisis broke, was afforded extensive amounts of protection and honor.[13] In *Truth and Repair: How Trauma Survivors Envision Justice*, Judith Herman describes Cardinal Law's treatment:

> Cardinal Law did find it convenient to get out of Boston for the friendly environs of the Vatican after the *Boston Globe's* Spotlight investigation revealed the depths of his complicity with these crimes, but he was never held accountable in any of the ways . . . survivors would have wished. He may not have kept his scepter and his big diamond ring, and he never did fulfill his rumoured lifelong

---

[12] Code of Canon Law, 1370.
[13] Laura Smith-Spark, "Pope's Role in Disgraced Cardinal's Funeral Draws Outrage," *CNN World* online, December 21, 2017.

ambition of becoming the first American pope, but he lived out his days in luxury and comfort in Rome, as the archpriest at the venerable Basilica of Santa Maria Maggiore, attended by nuns. When it comes to accountability for institutional enablers of criminal violence, we are a long way from survivors' justice.[14]

Cardinal Law did not need to sue the Church in order to be showered with wealth, and he was not asked to sign any nondisclosure agreements while fading away in silence. Rather, he was given a prince's funeral with the pope offering his final benediction. There have been victims of CPSA who have died by suicide as a result of their trauma, yet clericalist culture still protects and honors the abusive clerics more than the victims whose deaths it has cultivated. It is clear that when ordained ministry is understood through the lens of substance ontology, the Church believes its abusive ministers deserve honor and protection more than the abused laity deserve justice because the abusive ministers are substantially set apart as more valuable than lay persons.

In the first chapter, we argued that it is common for Catholic sacramental theology to overemphasize the liturgy as a *source* of grace to the detriment of seeing the liturgy as the *summit* of grace. Understanding ordained ministry through a framework of substance ontology is tantamount to an overemphasis on the liturgy as the source of grace. This reliance on substance ontology reinforces the notion that ordained clergy are the sole mediators of God's grace. They become perceived as gatekeepers of salvation. In turn, substance ontology contributes to and perpetuates a clericalist culture by elevating the clergy to a position of exclusive power and authority. Just as no one

---

[14] Judith L. Herman, *Truth and Repair: How Trauma Survivors Envision Justice* (London: Basic Books, 2023), 136.

should deny that the liturgy is a source of grace, our purpose is not to deny the existence of a substance ontology. Rather, when substance ontology is overemphasized and allowed to become the primary way ordained ministers are understood and treated, then clericalism is at work. Within the framework of substance ontology, all the focus is placed on the fact that ministers *have* the power instead of *how* they received the power, *why* ministers have the power, or what they can *accomplish* with the power. These latter considerations turn our focus from a substance ontology to a relational ontology.

Ordained Ministry Rooted in Relational Ontology

According to Pope Francis, if clericalism is to be avoided, then the vocation of ordained ministry must be seen "as a free and generous service to be given."[15] Put differently, rather than preoccupation with the power clerics have (that is, the indelible character), the Church should primarily focus on the task to which God has called them (that is, service to the body of Christ). To work against the threats that clericalism poses to the Church and to avoid further cases of abuse and cover-up, there must be a shift from an ordained ministry rooted in a substance ontology to one rooted in a relational ontology.

Fundamental to a relational ordained ministry is the understanding that ordained ministry is a gift continually given by God through the agency of the entire people of God, including the laity.[16] There must be a recognition that ordained ministry is in service of the laity's mission to be the presence

---

[15] Pope Francis, "Address by His Holiness Pope Francis at the Opening of the Synod of Bishops on Young People, the Faith and Vocational Discernment."

[16] Richard R. Gaillardetz, *By What Authority? Foundations for Understanding Authority in the Church*, rev. and exp. ed. (Collegeville, MN: Liturgical Press, 2018).

of Christ to the world. Known as the baptismal priesthood or the priesthood of the faithful, all the baptized are called and sent to be the mediating presence of Christ's love and justice to the world. The entire purpose of the ministerial priesthood is to support this mission of the baptismal priesthood.[17] Put differently, the ministerial priesthood receives its unique call through the needs of the baptismal priesthood. Gaillardetz emphasizes this point by reflecting on the fact that, according to the Second Vatican Council, clerics are ordained "in the person of Christ the Head."[18] However, he points out that "head" here should not be understood hierarchically, but instead as the leadership of service. Gaillardetz writes, "The priest is 'head' as Christ is 'head,' not as one to be served but as one called to serve; not as one whose feet should be washed, but as one who washes the feet of others."[19]

So, while the priesthood of the baptized and the priesthood of the ordained are distinct, they are inseparable. Strictly speaking, then, the substance ontology we rehearsed in the previous section cannot exist without its relationship to the rest of the Church. Put differently, the ordained ministry has no substance that is independent of the laity and the baptismal priesthood. Any clericalist theology of ordained ministry that seeks to isolate and elevate ordained ministers into a separate, elite caste has fundamentally misunderstood the nature of Christian priesthood.

---

[17] Kimberly Hope Belcher and Christopher M. Hadley, "Relational Priesthood in the Body of Christ: A Scriptural, Liturgical, and Trinitarian Approach," *Religions* 12, no. 10 (2021): 799. See also Jean-Pierre Torrell, *A Priestly People: A Baptismal Priesthood and Priestly Ministry* (New York: Paulist Press, 2013); and Paul Philibert, *The Priesthood of the Faithful: Key to a Living Church* (Collegeville, MN: Liturgical Press, 2005).

[18] Pope Paul VI, *Presbyterorum Ordinis* (*Decree on the Ministry and Life of Priests*), #2. See Richard Gaillardetz, "A Church in Crisis: How Did We Get Here? How Do We Move Forward?" *Worship* 70, no. 4 (December 2018): 214.

[19] Gaillardetz, 214.

In essence, the baptismal and the ministerial priesthood work together to form one active participation in the priesthood of Christ. This single priesthood is fundamentally a relational existence (that is, a relational ontology). Just as parenthood is a relational ontology constituted by the dynamic and interdependent relationships between parents and children, so too, the one priesthood of the Church is constituted by the simultaneous interaction of the ordained ministers and the entire people of God. In their exposition of the relational nature of ordained ministry, Catholic theologians Kimberly Belcher and Christopher Hadley emphasize that the one Christian priesthood cannot be properly understood as the sole activity of the clergy, much less the activity of an individual cleric: "Christian priesthood is exercised by the people of God unitively, not by ordained priests towards the baptized from which they are ontologically distinct, but rather mutually, interdependently, and by means of encounter."[20]

Adopting a theology of ordained ministry that is rooted in a relational ontology will have tangible effects on the culture of the Catholic Church. As Gaillardetz argues, this ministry will be recognizable by consistent acts of solidarity with the laity.[21] Specifically, there should be acts of ongoing solidarity with the particular community that the ordained minister is serving. A parish priest should spend the vast majority of his time with the members of the parish, not just within the walls of the church building during liturgies but in the surrounding community and in the homes of the people whom he strives to serve. Similarly, the laity should take seriously their responsibility to collaborate with and support ordained ministers. During the ordination liturgies, the person being ordained will consistently be prayed for by the entire assembly. In one particularly moving moment, the ordinand lies prostrate on the floor while the assembly sings

---

[20] Belcher and Hadley, "Relational Priesthood in the Body of Christ," 799.
[21] Gaillardetz, "A Church in Crisis," 218.

the litany of saints, interceding on behalf of the minister and the whole Church. This prayerful support should not cease after the ordination. As the sex-abuse crisis clearly attests, those who are ordained to support and lead the Church are incapable of living up to their vocation on their own and are in constant need of aid—aid that they must receive in large part from the laity.

Similarly, a bishop should build relationships with the communities of his diocese. Gaillardetz highlights the fact that, in the early centuries of the Church's history, there was a clear belief in "the right of the local Church to affirm, either by election or acclamation, the appointment of their bishop."[22] Further, the notion that bishops would be moved from one diocese to another was seen as contrary to the nature of the episcopacy. Bishops were meant to be overseers of a particular geographic area. They were meant to have an intimate knowledge of the people they were serving.[23] According to Catholic sacramental theologian Adam DeVille: "One is always therefore ordained for, and thus enters into a lifelong commitment to, a particular church (parish or diocese) in a particular place, and never as a 'freelancer' or a vagrant."[24] When a cleric is accountable to a single community, they are allowed a greater opportunity to dedicate themselves to the community wherein they reside and build a stronger foundation of connections, something critical to the mental health and well-being of all individuals. When a minister is connected to their community through concrete and habitual acts of solidarity, the cleric's social support systems become stronger as they are able to be aided by their community in times of need. The ability to ask for help humanizes a priest and strengthens the unity and grace within the body of the Church, further working against the culture of poisonous

---

[22] Gaillardetz, 218.
[23] DeVille, "The Sacrament of Orders Dogmatically Understood."
[24] DeVille.

isolation and secrecy that is demanded by clericalism. By emphasizing a relational ontology, the Church is more likely to see *Lumen Gentium*'s vision of robust collaboration come to fruition, wherein "all according to their proper roles may cooperate in this common undertaking with one mind" (*LG*, #30).

In today's Church the emphasis on a bishop's relationship to the particular local church he is serving has, in many ways, given way to a never-ending series of promotions that moves a bishop from one diocese to another based on his performance and favor with the bishops who are more powerful than he. In essence, the relationships that really matter to a bishop's identity are his relationships to the other bishops, especially the pope. When an ordained minister's relationships to his local Church community are ignored in preference for his relationships to his fellow ordained ministers, a relational ontology has been abandoned for a substance ontology: a clear symptom of a clericalist culture. Ideally, then, each particular ordained minister's identity and authority are derived from and determined by his relationship to the particular laity or their community. Catholic theologian Serena Noceti remarks on the importance of the lay collaboration beautifully:

> [The laity] are not to be seen as simply obedient executors of instructions given by clergy nor as mere collaborators in pastoral work for which they are not truly responsible. Nor should they be considered passive recipients of doctrinal formation that only ordained ministers can offer; rather, they possess a vision of reality and a spiritual experience that must be recognized and welcomed so that the work of evangelization of the life of the church can be fulfilled.[25]

---

[25] Serena Noceti, *Reforming the Church: A Synodal Way of Proceeding* (New York: Paulist Press, 1989), 30.

So, when Pope Francis says in his 2018 opening address to the Synod on Young People that the vocation of ordained ministry must be seen "as a free and generous service to be given," we might add that it should be seen as a service that must be continually *received* if it is going to be freely and generously given. The power to be a good and effective minister is not one that is fully accomplished at an ordination. A good minister's ability to minister must be cultivated by ongoing relationships with the people of God. In the end, when we choose to adopt a lens of a relational ontology, we come to see that even the characteristics that are emphasized by substance ontology do not actually exist independently of the minister's relationships to the rest of the Church. As Aquinas points out, even the indelible character of holy orders is a sign that points to a relational ontology. An ordained minister is sealed with an indelible character because he now exists for the purpose of serving the Church and the faithful.[26] We should recall that the instruments given to a priest during his ordination are the chalice and the paten, not bread and wine. In other words, the instruments that were for centuries the essential matter of ordination are instruments used to *nourish the laity*. The purpose of these instruments is not fulfilled when the bread and wine are consecrated. Their purpose (and, therefore, the purpose of the ordained minister) is fulfilled when the Eucharist is eaten by the congregation, nourishing them for their work as Christ's presence to the world.

Preventing Abuse and Healing Trauma through Relational Ordained Ministry

How does a theology of ordained ministry that is rooted in a relational ontology help address systemic CPSA and its

---

[26] Thomas Aquinas, *Summa Theologiae*, III, Q. 63, A. 1, co.

consequences? First, this approach to ministry helps dismantle the metaphysics on which the clericalist culture that creates and sustains abusive practices like systemic CPSA rests. If an ordained minister's identity is fundamentally derived from the diocese or parish he is serving, it becomes more difficult to clandestinely move abusive priests and bishops from one parish or diocese to another. Moving abusive priests from one parish to another proved to be particularly indicative of the ongoing systemic cover-up. Parishes were not warned about the history of the priests being relocated to their community, and they were left vulnerable to ongoing cases of assault. In the case of bishops, seeing certain dioceses as more prestigious than others (for example, New York; Washington, DC; and Chicago) encourages a form of careerism, wherein a bishop might seek to protect his reputation so that he is a more promotable candidate. If, on the other hand, a bishop must come from and remain tied to the same diocese throughout his career, he might be less likely to treat the community as a flock of sheep that have been momentarily entrusted to him as he is passing through on his way to greener pastures.

Second, adopting a relational ontology bolsters the dignity of both the laity and the ordained. Instead of treating laity as passive members of an inferior caste (that is, as sheep), the laity's lives of sacrifice are seen as the purpose through which God calls the clergy to lives of service. The laity are more likely to be seen by themselves *and by the clergy* as instruments of God's grace and as active collaborators whose baptismal priesthood is the essential and inextricable collaborator of the ministerial priesthood. As such, the unique dignity of each diocese, each parish, and each lay person is seen as integral to God's salvific activity in history.

Further, a relational ontology highlights the dignity of ordained ministers. Within a relational ontology, these leaders cannot be reduced to their indelible sacramental character; they cannot be defined by their liturgical capacities to preside, consecrate, and absolve. Instead of being erased, their unique talents and personalities are seen as gifts God has granted them through their relationships to both the laity and other clergy. Ministers' talents are then used by God to best serve the part of the Church where they minister. In these ways, when a lay or ordained person's diverse relationships are appreciated as the source and summit of their very being, their dignity is upheld and allowed to flourish. The dehumanizing, commodifying, and idolatrous tendencies of clericalism are avoided insofar as all members of the Church are celebrated as full participants in the saving mission of Christ.

Third, when a priest's authority and power are understood as a relationship that is given through the agency of the laity, the ordained minister is less likely to be fetishized and idolized. In other words, they are more likely to be respected and valued for the uniquely gifted individuals they truly are and not for the powerful caste they represent. Because the clergy are no longer imagined to be separated and elevated members of a holier echelon, they no longer provoke the deference that accompanies lay members' sense of inferiority. This means that the laity will rightly be less instinctively and subconsciously docile in response to clerical authority. There is no shortage of testimonies from CPSA survivors that highlight the fact that abusive priests were often seen as beyond criticism, leading to survivors facing barriers to reporting the abuse and/or people not believing the survivors when they were able to tell their stories. For example, recalling his attempt to seek help when he was abused as a thirteen-year-old boy, David Nolan recalls that, "We put them (priests) on pedestals almost to the point where I thought they were more than superhuman in a sense."[27] When Nolan decided to seek help from the police, he was dismissively laughed at by the police and then coerced by his assailant into recanting his testimony. Like many people who hold positions of extreme power and prestige, priests who are afforded a divine status are consistently and detrimentally given the benefit of the doubt. When allowed to reform one's imagination, a relational ontology can remove the tendency to see ordained ministers as idols and start seeing them as the fallible yet dignified individuals they are.

Last, a framework of relational ontology for ordained ministry removes the sense of impunity that many priests and (especially) bishops enjoy, instead insisting on accountability.[28] If a cleric's sense of impunity derives from his sense of being an exclusive conduit for God's grace and authority, then adopting a relational ontology can help erode this idolatrous self-perception. Adopting a keen awareness of his indebtedness to those he is called to serve should rid a cleric of any narcissistic belief that he is beyond critique "from below." Rather, when ministers take their accountability to the laity seriously, they should consistently seek to assess their vocational success by seeking input from those they serve. When we understand the authority of ordained ministers as a gift that is continually given by God through the agency of the lay community, the power imbalances that enabled systemic CPSA are more easily subverted.

Further, one can hope that a relational view of ordained ministry will result in a genuine form of shared governance in

---

[27] In Muhammad, "Catholic Church Accused of Denying Justice to Blacks Abused by Priests."

[28] James F. Keenan, "Hierarchicalism," *Theological Studies* 83, no. 1 (2022): 84–108.

which the laity are no longer relegated to advisory roles. The fact that Pope Francis's decision to grant a small number of lay people voting rights during a 2023 meeting of the Synod of Bishops was met with so much publicity and controversy is indicative of just how little accountability the bishops are willing to accept. The Church is currently a far cry from its past practices of taking the will of the lay people seriously.[29] As such, the laity should continue to utilize every secular avenue at their disposal to truncate the impunity of clerics.[30] When clericalism continues to marginalize the laity from any meaningful role in governing the Church, forcibly holding clergy accountable is a necessary and concrete reminder of the relational ontology many clericalists would like to forget.

Importantly, a relational approach to ordained ministry helps heal the consequences of CPSA that are damaging the liturgy's ability to work. First, as we described in the third and fourth chapters, regardless of a particular minister's guilt or innocence, his mere presence can trigger flashbacks and/or provoke a sense of betrayal in a person suffering from PTSD and/or moral injury. The substance ontology of clericalism exacerbates the symptoms that are triggered by an ordained minister. The more that ordained ministers are reduced to their indelible character and treated like interchangeable symbols, the more their significance is contaminated by the Church's history of abuse. In other words, within a substance ontology,

---

[29] Gaillardetz, "A Church in Crisis," 218.

[30] For example, the work of the *Boston Globe*'s Spotlight team to uncover the systemic cover-up of CPSA in the Archdiocese of Boston is a shining example of lay people insisting on accountability. There are many other lay organizations and individuals whose tireless work, often undertaken with backlash from the Catholic Church, has done much to hold the Church's ordained ministers accountable, for example, The Survivors Network of Those Abused by Priests, BishopAccountability.Org; and Ending Clergy Abuse.

these interchangeable men are more easily condemned through guilt by association because clericalism insists that they are essentially, functionally, and substantially the same. If a relational ontology were to be adopted and the unique histories, talents, and personalities of each minister allowed to define his role as a priest or bishop, then the conduct of ordained ministers, whether good or bad, might be less likely to reflect so intensely on the other members of the ministerial priesthood. By no longer treating ministers as interchangeable symbols, the Church would cultivate a safer space for people struggling with PTSD and moral injury. The result would be liturgies that are less likely to be experienced as dehumanizing violence or as hollow acts of hypocrisy. Instead, the liturgy might be better able to fruitfully communicate God's love and friendship.

Second, by emphasizing a relational ontology, the agency of the laity is more fully acknowledged and fostered. The fact that, by virtue of their baptism, all the laity are instruments of God's salvation emphasizes the indispensability of their cooperation with ordained ministers. Because PTSD, moral injury, and moral distress all have deleterious effects on a person's agency, any framework that helps to recognize and affirm the importance of a lay person's agency can help mitigate these shadows of trauma. For example, adopting a relational ontology can assuage the feelings of powerlessness that a lay person might feel as a result of moral injury and/or moral distress. A relational approach to ordained ministry works against the feeling of powerlessness because the laity are more readily aware of the ways that their agency has and continues to influence the culture of the Church. This shift may not do away with a person's sense of complicity in the clericalist culture, but it will mitigate the sense of powerlessness, hopefully avoiding hopelessness and resignation. As such, the consequences of moral injury and moral distress that hinder liturgical efficacy can be mitigated, opening the possibility of a fruitful experience of liturgy. In the end, embracing a theology of ordained ministry that is rooted in a relational ontology both helps heal the harmful consequences of systemic CPSA *and* helps reform the abusive culture of clericalism. Both the symptoms and the disease can be addressed.

Conclusion: The Gift of Authority

We conclude our examination of the way theologies of ordained ministry can affect how clericalism and systemic CPSA influence the liturgy with a liturgical story that beautifully expresses the power of ordained ministry rooted in a relational ontology. This is a personal story of an Orthodox priest's final liturgy with the parish community whom he had served as pastor for thirty-seven years, after having initially been a member of the parish as a lay person before attending seminary. The liturgy was a celebration of this man's retirement, and it was a packed service. In addition to the many friends and family members attending the liturgy, a bishop and the dean of the deanery were present (both of whom outranked the retiring priest). They had traveled across states to concelebrate the liturgy as a way of honoring this man's life of ordained ministry. When it came time for the rite of communion, the priest took a place in the middle of the nave, while the visiting ministers stood nearer to the altar. The assembly had three options for where they could receive communion: the bishop, the dean, or their pastor of thirty-seven years, whose adult son was standing beside him to assist in distributing communion.

Unsurprisingly, as communion began, almost every person in the church moved to stand in the priest's communion line. Almost immediately, the two visiting ministers were left standing quietly and alone, while the priest's line was full of people patiently waiting to be fed by his hand. After a few brief moments, the priest noticed what was happening. Visibly agitated, he paused the distribution of communion and addressed the assembly, encouraging them to go to the bishop or the dean to receive communion. "Some of you, please go to the other lines. It is all the same presence of Christ we are receiving." He spoke kindly and clearly. Everyone heard, and no one moved. The bishop and the dean continued to stand unmoving, and the priest's line slowly progressed as he fed them each from the chalice being held by his son. Undoubtedly, the members of his parish meant no disrespect to the visiting ministers. The bishop and the dean were not being ignored; the pastor was being loved. It was a beautiful and moving celebration of communion.

This liturgy teaches at least two lessons. First, the power and authority of an ordained minister is a gift that is continually given through the agency of the assembly. On most days in a bishop's life, his presence at a liturgy is worthy of note. Yet here, the rare presence of the bishop was clearly not as important or meaningful as the presence of the priest. The members of the parish disobeying the priest's plea to receive communion from the bishop was a shining example of how a minister's authority is a gift that can very easily and very rightly be denied by thoughtful members of the laity. And this priest responded wonderfully: he accepted their unwillingness to obey and continued serving them to the best of his ability. He did not get angry and repeat himself in an attempt to assert his authority. As a thoughtful priest, he knew it was not *his* authority to exercise. Rather, his authority was a dynamic relationship of love between him and the members of his parish.

The second lesson learned from this liturgy is that the presence of Christ in the liturgy is a dynamic and personal encounter that is expressed through the unique relationships among the members of the Church. When asking that some members of the assembly receive communion from the bishop and the dean, the priest appealed to the notion that "it is all the same presence of Christ." Essentially saying, "Whether you receive the Eucharist from me or from the bishop, you are still receiving the same real presence of Jesus." This is good, traditional eucharistic theology. When the bread and wine are consecrated, Jesus is truly present. Indeed, some might hear this story and scold the assembly for being too focused on their relationship to the pastor when they should have been focusing on their relationship to Jesus, who was equally present in each instance of the Eucharist. However, we argue that the pastor's claim that it was "all the same" is incorrect. Clearly, the friends and family of the pastor wanted to encounter Christ in a way that made them feel alive with the love of God. Because an ordained minister is meant to be a representation of Christ's presence, the assembly was more able to recognize the pastor as such precisely because of the way he had loved them for decades. The unique histories he shared with each person surrounded the consecrated bread and wine as he fed them, utterly saturating the moment with so much meaning that the Christ they encountered through his presence was a different Christ than the one they would have encountered being fed by the bishop.

To be clear, we are not arguing that Jesus was "more" present in the bread and wine distributed by the pastor. Nor are we arguing that Jesus's presence was "better" when coming from the pastor's chalice. Rather, we are arguing that a relational ontology of ordained ministry eclipses the minimalist ontologies that are preoccupied with substance and character. The fact that, due to their consecration, the other men were powerful ministers of a higher rank simply did not have as much meaning as the power of the pastor's love. In this story we see a clear picture of ordained ministry rooted in relational ontology; it was the antithesis of clericalism. The presence of the bishop was meant to be an honor to the retiring pastor, and it undeniably was a kind and thoughtful gesture. Yet the strongest honor shown to the pastor came through the disobedience of his friends and family. They refused to be separated from him because they longed to feel the presence of Christ's love mediated through all the memories of his love for them. And, being a humble and patient minister, he did not deny them.

If the relational ontology of ordained ministers is allowed to fundamentally shape the way the Church understands, forms, and treats its clergy, then the clericalist culture of death will struggle to persist. Through the liturgy, Jesus insists that all of his followers have a role to play in the salvation of the world. When an ordained ministry rooted in a relational ontology is embraced, then the liturgy should become all the more a *communal* celebration wherein each member of the entire congregation is a full, active participant. The liturgical passivity and deference that would usually cultivate the clericalist minister gives way to a robust call for contributions from the laity. In the face of pain, fear, guilt, powerlessness, and resignation, the liturgy (when competently and passionately led by a minister whose actions are grounded in personal relationships with the people he serves) will be better able to provocatively call to them, pleading with them to use their agency.

7

Avoiding Rhetorical Violence

> *Let me state it bluntly: the Eucharist is the single most important reason for staying faithful to the Church. You can't find it anywhere else; and no wickedness on the part of priests or bishops can affect it.*[1]
>
> —BISHOP ROBERT BARRON

Too often, Catholics who are struggling with post-traumatic stress disorder (PTSD), moral injury, or moral distress that can arise from exposure to systemic clergy perpetrated sexual abuse (CPSA) are confronted with manipulative rhetoric that insists on their continued participation in liturgical life of the Church. Catholic leaders speak and write in ways that expect forgiveness and describe the liturgical life of the Church as an obligation for everyone, regardless of the abuse they've endured. In this chapter we explore the ways that people living in the shadows of systemic CPSA continue to be abused by the violent rhetoric used by Catholic leaders. When someone is abused, the person is often manipulated by the abuser as a means to keeping the survivor close. The same is true of

---

[1] Bishop Robert Barron, *Letter to a Suffering Church: A Bishop Speaks on the Sexual Abuse Crisis* (Park Ridge, IL: Word on Fire, 2019), 74.

systemic CPSA. To stop Catholics from leaving the Church, Catholic leaders employ rhetoric that manipulates the emotions of survivors. As we will show, this is especially true when it comes to the liturgy. In this way clericalist culture functions as a cycle of abuse that manipulates survivors into remaining part of a flock that belongs to the clergy.

Cycles of Abuse and Rhetorical Manipulation

As we have highlighted in previous chapters, the language and symbols that a community uses to communicate have an immense influence on the development of that community's identity (that is, their values and behaviors).[2] Catholic moral theologian A. Denise Starkey has pointed out that Roman Catholic rhetoric regarding sin and confession can amplify the experience of shame that many survivors of domestic abuse experience.[3] Rhetoric, especially coming from a place of power and control, shapes individuals' understanding of themselves, others, and their place in the world. Hence, rhetoric can become violent when it imbues a person or a community with messages of unworthiness, sinfulness, and subjugation. For many people who have been harmed by systemic CPSA, these messages can instill a sense of guilt and shame, exacerbating one's experience of PTSD, moral injury, and moral distress. Clericalist culture teaches people that salvation is unattainable without liturgical participation and obedience to Church authority. This dynamic traps individuals in a cycle of abuse.

---

[2] For example, see Hilary Jerome Scarsella, "Victimization via Ritualization: Christian Communion and Sexual Abuse," in *Trauma and Lived Religion: Transcending the Ordinary*, ed. R. Ruard Ganzevoort and Srjdan Sremac (Cham, Switzerland, 2018), 240.

[3] A. Denise Starkey, *The Shame That Lingers: A Survivor-Centered Critique of Catholic Sin-Talk* (Lausanne, Switzerland: Peter Lang Group AG, 2009).

To better understand the cyclic nature of abusive cultures, we must first turn to the role of emotions. According to professor of criminology Joan Reid, "trauma bonding" describes a psychological effect of abuse in which a person forms an emotional attachment to their abuser.[4] This emotional bond is often the result of intermittent reinforcements of kindness, care, or hope amid the harm caused by an abuser.[5] After abusing someone, the abuser may be apologetic and make the survivor feel uniquely loved and special. When someone's repeated abuse is broken up by intermittent kindness and care, they are often being taught to associate their suffering with love. Hence, a survivor may develop powerful feelings of desire to have the love and approval of their abuser. This can lead them to seek ongoing proximity to their abuser whether that abuser is an individual, a group, or a culture. For many who escape a cycle of abuse and find themselves in healthy relationships, the lack of intense emotions that comes along with abuse can feel like the healthy relationship is broken or lacking. These powerful emotions become leverage for an abuser in their quest to manipulate and control a person so that they can maintain ownership over them. As a result, survivors are often more susceptible to being manipulated back into the intense cycle of abuse.

Many of these tactics of manipulation are akin to the ways that clericalist culture is used to maintain control of the members of the Catholic Church who may want to disaffiliate due to their experiences of systemic CPSA.[6] The process of

---

[4] Joan A. Reid, *Trauma Bonding and Interpersonal Crimes* (Hoboken, NJ: John Wiley and Sons, 2024), 1–5.

[5] Reid, 1.

[6] It must be noted that systemic CPSA is not the only form of abuse that Catholic culture inflicts on people. Women and members of the LGBTQIA+ community may also wish to disaffiliate due to a consistent experience of abuse that dehumanizes them (for example, repeatedly being told they are

navigating one's way out of an abusive relationship is riddled with complexity and conflicting emotions. These powerful emotions of attachment are not easily severed, because they operate through a deeply ingrained belief system that is reinforced by years of indoctrination and cultural conditioning.[7]

For many, the decision to leave an abusive relationship does not happen all at once but rather unfolds over time as they reconcile feelings of betrayal, fear, and loss with a desire for healing and autonomy. While grappling with the abuse that they have endured, they also experience the grief of potentially losing their community or loss of rituals and traditions that bring comfort and guidance. The duality of grief and relief is an all too common experience for people who are trying to navigate their way out of an abusive situation. These individuals often feel an ache for what was lost while simultaneously celebrating the liberation from an abusive system. If the Church cares about the health and flourishing of its members (especially the survivors of systemic CPSA), then it must refuse to manipulate these powerful emotions that perpetuate cycles of abuse. Seen through this lens, we can reiterate our often made point that abuse and trauma are not limited to events of acute, intense violence. Rather, acute abuse is often the result of ongoing abuse. Rhetorical manipulation *is* abuse, and it perpetuates the cycle of abuse.

---

intrinsically disordered, deformed, sinful, inadequate, and so on). These linguistic frameworks are reinforced by marginalization and exclusion from participation in the community, practices that degrade a person's agency over time. As such, trauma bonds can be exploited to manipulate survivors of other forms of abuse, as well.

[7] For example, when addressing the unique nature of trauma bonds that form within cults, a form of manipulation called "thought reform" often involves intricate and consistent control of a person's thoughts and feelings through control of the culture the person is exposed to. Cf. Reid, *Trauma Bonding and Interpersonal Crimes*, 131.

Rhetorical Manipulation and the Liturgy

How, then, does a clericalist culture manipulate the emotions of survivors to keep them in a cycle of abuse? Without trying to provide an exhaustive or systematic analysis of communications from Catholic leaders, this section highlights some examples of abusive rhetoric that perpetuate cycles of abuse. Our primary focus is on the way the liturgy (especially ordained ministry) is described as an obligation and as an exclusive source of salvation.

The liturgy is often presented as a pure source of grace that requires survivors to not lose hope. The liturgical theology of clericalist culture is used to maintain control by weaponizing hope and isolating survivors from sources of healing. This rhetoric is violent and abusive because it manipulates the emotions of survivors while simultaneously precluding any attempt at actual cultural reforms that would dismantle the clericalist culture that continues to perpetuate cycles of abuse. Clericalist culture uses rhetorical manipulation so that the survivor is more likely to stay affiliated with the Church and continue cultivating clericalism by participating in the liturgy. Here, we say that clericalist culture is the agent using rhetorical manipulation because most Catholic leaders are not intentionally engaging in abusive manipulation. Rather, their well-intentioned rhetoric and pastoral strategies are motivated by a desire to do what is best for the Church and for the laity. Of course, the same is true of nearly all abusers.

Rhetorically Weaponized Hope

"Weaponized hope" describes how a person's hope is manipulated to control their behavior. This is consistently seen in cycles of abuse when an abuser implies or explicitly demands that the survivor should forgive them and give them a second chance. After all, the argument goes, people can change and relationships can improve. Tactics that weaponize hope can be used in many different ways.

The liturgical life of the Church is often described in a way that asks Catholics to see the liturgy as something that deserves perpetual hope. Because the liturgy is supposed to provide a personal encounter with Christ, it is wrong to lose hope and turn your back on Christ. Throughout *A Letter to a Suffering Church*, Bishop Robert Barron repeatedly makes this argument. To do so, Barron heavily relies on the biblical metaphor of treasure in vessels. Taken from 2 Corinthians, Barron uses this metaphor to claim that what is good about a tradition (that is, the treasure) is separable from other parts of the tradition that might cause harm (that is, the vessels). Specifically, the grace of Christ (especially as experienced in the sacraments of the Church) is a "treasure" handed down through history by the "vessels" of the institutional structures of the Church.[8]

Similar to someone who says, "Don't throw the baby out with the bathwater," Barron is making the claim that the evils of systemic CPSA are extricable from the goodness of the liturgy. For Barron, sacraments like holy orders and the Eucharist are fundamentally pure treasures entrusted to the Church by Christ. Christ's salvation is dispensed to the world exclusively through the celebration of these sacraments, especially through the work and authority of the clergy.

By relying on the metaphor of treasure in a vessel, Barron is using a rhetorical device known as bracketing. When an issue is set aside and excluded from consideration, bracketing is being used as a means to distract attention from the clericalist

---

[8] Barron, *Letter to a Suffering Church*. It should be noted that while this chapter focuses most of its attention on Bishop Barron's rhetoric, he is by no means the only Catholic leader who speaks in these ways. The examples we highlight here are indicative of some of the most common ways that Catholic leaders tend to speak in response to systemic CPSA.

culture that he wishes to protect by maintaining the laity's participation in liturgical life of the Church. Throughout his letter, Barron grants attention only to insights and arguments that won't harm the clericalist culture he wants to protect. Instead, he shifts the focus to the "indestructible" goodness of the Church. This rhetoric leaves those harmed by systemic CPSA feeling as if they are wrong or misguided for questioning the Church and wanting to walk away from a clericalist culture that has caused so much pain. By holding up the liturgy as a pure "treasure," Barron seeks to provoke his readers' hope in a way that will allow them to tolerate the harm being done for the sake of the good being promised. He is weaponizing hope in a way that keeps people in a cycle of abuse.

As a rhetorical tactic, weaponizing hope also distracts people from the work of reform. Instead of focusing on the abusive culture that is causing so much harm, this manipulative rhetoric is used to placate readers' anger and draw their attention to a fantastical ideal that distracts from the abusive behavior. When addressing critiques that scrutinize the Church's clericalist culture, for example, Barron writes,

> I don't think for a moment that a change in its [the priesthood's] essential structure is called for. In my judgment, it is naive in the extreme to imagine that allowing priests to marry or women to be priests will greatly ameliorate this situation.[9]

Instead he calls for a "rededication to its [the priesthood's] ideals."[10] Barron quickly dismisses critics of the Catholic Church's traditional teachings on ordained ministry by calling them naive. Further, he associates concerns about clericalism

---

[9] Barron, 89–90.
[10] Barron, 89–90.

with controversial issues, such as whether or not priests should be able to marry or whether or not women can be ordained. By doing this, Barron shifts readers' attention back to the doctrinal ideals of ordained ministry. Rather than focusing attention on the reality of abuse that has arisen out of clericalist culture, Barron describes ordination in a way that establishes it as a pure treasure that only the extremely naive would dare to criticize.

In essence, Barron is overemphasizing the liturgy as a source that dispenses grace instead of focusing on the way it has clearly functioned as a source and summit of abuse. Focusing on an idealized version of ordained ministry affords him more control over the conversation and further distracts attention from the abusive clericalist culture. He is willing to question, examine, or entertain criticism of the clericalist structures within the Church only as long as those critiques do not affect the theologies of ordained ministry that grant him and his fellow clergy the immense power they enjoy. In other words, by provoking hope in an idealized vision of the liturgy, he is able to divert critical questioning away from clericalism so that clericalism can continue to operate unaddressed. As we described in the second and sixth chapters, clericalist ideals of the priesthood (for example, a theology of ordained ministry rooted in a substance ontology) have created a culture in which abuse can thrive, but, by holding our attention on a reaffirmation of and rededication to clericalist ideals, Barron does not have to respond to horrors that occur when those ideals are put in action.

Rhetorical manipulation occurs through weaponized hope because the very weaponization of hope concentrates a survivor's emotions on the fantasy of a pure, incorruptible liturgy. Their love and loyalty are stirred up in a way that demands their hope and forgiveness. One example of this rhetoric comes from a pastoral letter to the Catholics of Ireland written by Pope Benedict XVI in March 2010. In this letter the pope exhorts those suffering the effects of systemic CPSA to not leave the Church:

> I ask you not to lose hope. It is in the communion of the Church that we encounter the person of Jesus Christ.... I know some of you find it difficult even to enter the doors of a church after all that has occurred. Yet Christ's own wounds, transformed by his redemptive sufferings, are the very means by which the power of evil is broken and we are reborn to life and hope.

While this is a good example of a proper acknowledgment of the difficulties facing survivors, the pope fails to avoid weaponizing hope. To rekindle lost hope in a healthy manner, one should not invite a survivor back to the site of their abuse. Instead, Catholic leaders ought to be taking responsibility for lost hope and encouraging survivors and those affected by CPSA to take time to heal, even condoning healing that must occur outside of the Church. But this is not the messaging we tend to hear from Catholic leaders. Rather, the exhortation to maintain hope in the face of one's abuser and to keep coming back to the site of the abuse for the sake of one's salvation, which is offered solely through one's abuser, sets survivors up to be judged erroneously as failures if they ultimately do "lose hope" and pull away from the Church. This rhetoric weaponizes the hope of the survivor, such that the survivor is implicitly blamed for failing to maintain it. It implies that the survivor is not doing enough, not healing correctly, and turning away from a salvation offered exclusively by an institution that is deeply harming them. The result is the exploitation of powerful emotions that manipulates survivors into remaining in an abusive culture.

Rhetorical Isolation

By provoking strong emotional connections to the liturgy and ordained ministers, weaponized hope is a powerful tactic that uses a person's love and loyalty against them, drawing them deeper into the cycle of abuse. A similarly powerful form of emotional manipulation comes from provoking fear of outsiders in order to isolate someone. Isolation is a common tactic of abusers that ensures outside influences cannot compromise the abuser's control. To conclude this section, then, we focus on how rhetorical manipulation is used to isolate Catholics who are struggling with the consequences of systemic CPSA. If people believe that they have no other options, the cycle of abuse is more likely to continue.

One egregious example of rhetorical isolation from Bishop Barron's book comes when he writes: "Let me state it bluntly: the Eucharist is the single most important reason for staying faithful to the Church. You can't find it anywhere else; and no wickedness on the part of priests or bishops can affect it."[11] Falsely insisting that the Eucharist is not available anywhere else is an exploitation of the survivor's love for the liturgy.[12] It is weaponized hope. This type of rhetoric doesn't just try to provoke hope; it demands hope as an obligation. Instead of leaving, the abused person is expected to forgive the Church and hope that things will get better. Further, by denying the existence of the Eucharist elsewhere, Barron employs a thinly

---

[11] Barron, 74.

[12] In the next chapter we show precisely why Barron's claim is contrary to Catholic teaching, especially that of the Second Vatican Council.

veiled scare tactic that is meant to make Catholics doubt the salvific presence of Christ in the eucharistic celebrations of other Christian communities.[13] Like an abuser who says, "No one will ever love you the way I do," Barron's message is meant to exert control; regardless of how abusive Catholic leaders may become, every Catholic must remain in the flock and hope that the cycle of abuse will stop.

Relying on substance ontology to describe and frame the ordained ministry is a rhetorical technique that functions to isolate the people they are trying to control. When the Catholic Church insists upon interchangeable clerics as the *only* source of forgiveness and healing, it is essentially mimicking the behavior of abusers who isolate their victims. Hence, in the cycle of abuse, where degradation and violence are interspersed with kindness and care, the survivor can develop a sense of gratitude and affection for the abuser precisely because they are isolated and kept from recognizing other relationships as possible avenues of healing and flourishing. This isolation can occur physically (for example, the Catholic Church's removal of Indigenous children from their homes and placing them in schools far from their families), but it can also occur linguistically when other people, communities, or cultures are described as inadequate, deficient, sinful, or threatening. This isolation forces survivors to identify the abusive culture as the source of their salvation.

When Catholic leaders try to equate acute abusive behaviors with unfortunate sins that are not intrinsic to Catholic culture, while maintaining the "purity" of the Church's ordained ministry as the true source of salvation, they are essentially teaching survivors that ordained ministers are their best and only source of healing and salvation. Barron, for example,

---

[13] For more on why Barron's claim that "you can't find [the Eucharist] anywhere else" is factually inaccurate, see the first chapter of this book.

goes so far as to write: "There is simply never a good reason to leave the Church. Never."[14] As is the case with many abusers, this type of language is used to manipulate emotions in a way that draws people closer to the abuser's sphere of influence. Framing a person or a culture as unorthodox, heretical, blasphemous, or dangerous can be a powerful way of excluding alternative sources of healing that might compromise a survivor's connection to the abusive authority figure.

When a Catholic leader incites fear and weaponizes hope against people who are struggling with the effects of systemic CPSA, they are essentially asking the people to sacrifice their own healing to the idol of clerical power. Of course, most of these clerics intend to keep the laity in relationship with Christ's Church, a relationship they genuinely believe will benefit the laity. These good intentions are not unique or exculpatory. Most abusers genuinely believe their controlling and abusive behavior is good for the people they abuse. Yet, it is both unreasonable and harmful to request that someone reenter the context that harmed them in order to heal, and it is even more inappropriate to make such a request when the person making the request has done so little work to reform the culture that has caused such harm in the first place.

While there have been immense amounts of work and resources spent to find ways to protect people (for example, background checks, no tolerance policies, and so on) in the Catholic Church, this work should not be confused with the work of fundamentally reforming clericalist culture. Through the abusive rhetoric described above, Catholic leaders reinforce their own standing in the Church and shirk responsibility, making excuses for and downplaying the role of clericalism in CPSA. Then, instead of taking a real pastoral role in healing,

---

[14] Barron, *Letter to a Suffering Church*, 59.

they shift the expectations of forgiveness and hope onto the survivor, weaponizing hope in order to keep survivors close.

Rhetoric that describes the Roman Catholic Church's liturgical life as an obligation, as necessary for salvation, or as a source of grace that cannot be found elsewhere functions to isolate survivors by manipulating their emotions. It stops them from finding sources of healing and salvation that are not affiliated with the clericalist culture that has caused PTSD, moral injury, and moral distress. Many Catholic leaders have made it clear that they will not willingly let survivors go, at least not without denigrating them for leaving. The result of all of this abusive rhetoric is a Church with a cycle of abuse churning at its core. Once we begin to recognize the myriad ways this cycle of abuse is perpetuated, we must seek out ways to begin breaking that cycle.

A Step Forward: Seeking Safety and Empowerment

Given these harmful patterns of speech, it is important to develop strategies for avoiding such rhetorical violence. The rhetoric from Catholic leaders that we rehearsed above is clearly not intended to be abusive. However, once we become aware of the harm of our actions, we have a responsibility to hold ourselves accountable, take concrete steps to improve, and do whatever possible to repair the damage we have inflicted. To conclude this chapter, we borrow the principles of safety and empowerment from trauma-informed care to provide a preliminary framework for ways to speak about liturgy without manipulating emotions in a manner that perpetuates the cycle of abuse.[15] Creating an environment where someone is

---

[15] For a more extensive treatment of the various approaches to trauma-informed care, see the work of the Trauma Informed Care Implementation Resource Center. See also, David F. Turnbloom, et al., "Confronting Rhe-

not actively under an immediate threat of physical violence is not the same as creating a safe and empowering environment. This framework is intended to serve as an initial measure, but not a cure, for the healing of those who have been harmed by systemic CPSA and for the reform of the culture of clericalism. Choosing to speak about liturgy in ways that prioritize safety and empowerment can ultimately help build a Church that begins to prioritize the dignity and flourishing of every individual through its liturgical practices.

Essentially, prioritizing safety means working to free an environment from anything that will be perceived as a threat to one's physical, psychological, or spiritual safety. If an ordained minister knows that members of their congregation have been abused by clergy and that a white clerical collar could be a trigger for those people, the principle of safety would dictate that he choose not to wear the collar in their presence, instead selecting clothing that is familiar and comforting. Liturgically speaking, implementing the principle of safety might mean avoiding language of obligation that describes refusal to attend mass as a mortal sin that jeopardizes one's salvation. Instead of describing mass as an obligatory duty, the liturgy could be described as a gratuitous offering of God's unconditional love.

Similarly, prioritizing empowerment means choosing to celebrate and encourage a person's agency and strengths, refusing to label them as broken or as a problem to be fixed. Rather than treating people as helpless, passive sheep in need of guidance and healing, the principle of empowerment emphasizes the dignity of each person as an unconditionally loved child of God, an agent who has been made in the divine image. Liturgically speaking, Catholic leaders can empower the faithful by describing the liturgy as a communal activity that benefits

---

torical Violence in Response to the Catholic Sex Abuse Crisis," *Journal of Religion & Society* 25 (2023): 1–22.

from the unique contributions of each worshiper. The planning and celebration of each liturgy should involve the input and creativity of worshipers, especially those whose experiences of systemic CPSA have pushed them to the margins of the Church.

In order to fruitfully implement the principles of safety and empowerment, one must begin by listening to the people who have been directly affected by systemic CPSA. To facilitate healing and avoid further damage, the best way forward is one where the voices of survivors are not only heard but validated and treated as guides for further action. In other words, the way that a Catholic leader might define safety may not be how a person experiencing PTSD would define safety, and the gifts that a Catholic leader might want to recognize in a person may not be the gifts that person feels called to offer.

Adopting these principles of trauma-informed care must begin with active listening. For example, Fr. Tom Bolte, a whistleblower of abuse in the Archdiocese of Cincinnati, delivered a sermon one Sunday publicly condemning the diocese and denouncing CPSA and the cover-up he knew was taking place. After Fr. Bolte stood before his congregation and directly spoke of the need for centering the voices of survivors, one survivor remarked, "He [Fr. Bolte] has decided to treat us with the same dignity that Jesus Christ would if he were walking the earth today, and we think, set into motion what will ultimately result in some changes in this diocese."[16] Instead of protecting his superiors and his own place of power, Fr. Bolte chose to focus on the suffering of those who experienced CPSA, publicly naming the abuses and cover-up that had occurred. Fr. Bolte used his voice to prioritize the experiences of

---

[16] Julie O'Neil/WCPO, "Local Priest Cheered for His Role as Whistleblower: Cincinnati Archdiocese under Investigation," BishopAccountability.org, February 6, 2005.

those being abused. Instead of making manipulative excuses, he unconditionally acknowledged the failures of Catholic leaders. As a result, his listeners felt believed and affirmed.

Similarly, in an article published in *America* in 2000, Fr. Donald Cozzens emphasized the role of listening as a means to combat the crisis of clericalist culture:

> If dialogue is to be achieved—and it is desperately needed in this period of crisis—priests and bishops need to listen as members of a community of faith. This is a different kind of listening than many church leaders are accustomed to. It requires a certain attitude of heart, a readiness to suspend one's ecclesial role in the community, to bracket one's convictions and assumptions, and to listen so that one may be both informed and transformed. In other words, it requires that one surrender to the possibility of conversion to a deeper understanding, to a new vision of what might be.[17]

Here, Cozzens calls for a renewed focus on clergy as members of the community alongside the laity. By encouraging the clergy to let go of their controlling grip on authority, Cozzens prioritizes the safety and empowerment of the laity. His language seeks to level the hierarchical imbalance of clericalism that has contributed to systemic CPSA. By describing the clergy as "members of a community of faith" who should "suspend [their] ecclesial role," he employs rhetoric that mitigates the threatening and manipulative authority of clergy while simultaneously insisting that the laity have an authority of their own that demands respect. Indeed, Cozzens insists that the

---

[17] Donald Cozzens, "Facing the Crisis in the Priesthood," *America Magazine: The National Catholic Review* online, November 4, 2000.

voices of the laity might, in the end, be what save the clergy from their clericalist self-idolatry.

While listening to the voices of those affected by systemic CPSA is a crucial step in implementing the principles of safety and empowerment, survivors should never be expected or feel compelled to explain their trauma or be asked to contribute to the healing of an organization that so deeply wounded them. Fostering a space for those who have been affected by CPSA to be heard, as Cozzens does, empowers survivors to share their experience. This means recognizing and empowering their agency to speak plainly and openly, with their accounts being given the weight they deserve. However, if Catholic leaders presume that the Church is entitled to these accounts, agency is immediately undermined. Insights and advice from people who have been affected by systemic CPSA should be seen as gratuitous gifts, and those who choose not to be involved with the Church must be equally respected and valued. When people are treated with respect and dignity, the Church furthers its efforts toward creating a safer environment. Note the intentional use of *furthers* its efforts instead of *succeeds* in its efforts. These trauma-informed principles do not presuppose that when they are implemented the Church will immediately be healed or renewed. Rather, they are initial steps on the journey of reform and healing.

Often, in Catholic leaders' rhetorical responses to systemic CPSA, there is an underlying expectation that, once the abuse has been acknowledged and settlements have been reached, those who experienced systemic CPSA are obligated to remain in the Church. This expectation clearly undermines the agency of survivors. Empowerment means validating and accepting the authority of each person. Lying beneath the undermined agency that occurs when Catholic leaders demand that survivors stay loyal to clerical authority is an emphasis on the liturgy as the only way that one can experience healing and salvation. As we pointed out in the first chapter, a mechanistic understanding of the liturgy creates a culture where the liturgy is used as a harmful tool for control. In these contexts the liturgical life of the Church compounds clericalist attitudes and adds to the injuries that are experienced by those who suffer the consequences of systemic CPSA.

When the Church speaks about the liturgy using the principles of safety and empowerment, a renewed vision of the liturgy as the source and summit of grace emerges. Instead of a clericalist mechanism that dispenses grace, the liturgy is described as an unwavering offering of God's loving friendship. As we experience the liturgy as an offering to participate in God's grace, we can empower persons' agency as they respond to God's invitation to share in divine love. The liturgy becomes a provocative, yet safe, invitation—one that each individual can choose to accept, or not. Ultimately, when we see the liturgy in this light, we reinforce that God's love is unconditional and always being offered. It is no longer framed in the language of duty and obligation, no longer implying threats of shame and damnation. When the liturgy is described as an offering of God's participative grace, those who have been affected by systemic CPSA become less likely to feel manipulated and threatened by the liturgical life of the Church.

Implementing the principles of safety and empowerment means emphasizing that God's love is not earned and cannot be lost. Many survivors of systemic CPSA have been made to feel that they must endure their abuse because the liturgy and the clerics who control it were necessary to earn God's love. God was owed their loyalty, even if it meant being dehumanized by God's ministers. Instead, describing and celebrating the liturgy in language that prioritizes safety and empowerment offers assurance that God has not and will not abandon them and would never force them to earn God's love.

In September 2003, Sister Sally Butler delivered a parish talk in which she passionately defended the rights of survivors to be free of obligations and duties to the Church:

> There is much talk of forgiveness and healing. I ask you to wait.... Please do not tell the victims/survivors how to feel. Don't tell them to "get on with their lives." If Carlos [a survivor of CPSA] hates, he hates. And God loves him. If healing is in his path, he will work it out, but in his time and God's time. There are too many priests and sisters urging the victims to move toward healing.[18]

Here, Sister Butler beautifully implements the principles of safety and empowerment. When she validates the variety of reactions that survivors may experience due to their abuse, including emotions like hatred, she empowers their agency. By standing in solidarity with survivors and affirming their right to feel strong negative emotions, she shows a commitment to their safety. Further, she forcefully affirms that, despite what some bishops may say about people who leave the Church, God loves them unconditionally and will be a healing presence with or without the presence of ordained ministers.

When we become aware of the widespread suffering that has been caused by systemic CPSA and the impact that suffering is having on the liturgical life of the Church, we must choose our words carefully when speaking about the liturgy. Language that paints the liturgy as an obligation or a treasure found exclusively in the hands of Roman Catholic clergy

---

[18] Sister Sally Butler, "Talk at St. Hugh Parish Voice," speech transcription, BishopAccountability.org, September 22, 2003.

serves to control and harm those who have been harmed by systemic CPSA. In short, such liturgical language does not empower the laity, nor does it make them any safer.

Our goal in this chapter has been to elucidate the harmful role that rhetoric can play in cultivating a cycle of abuse, while also indicating some ways that rhetoric might be employed to transform an abusive culture into one that better appreciates the persistent roots of abuse and the far-reaching consequences of trauma. The effects wrought by rhetoric are not always intentional. What a leader says and how a leader says it will affect the community in ways, both profound and subtle, that cannot always be controlled. Further, the influence of rhetoric is not limited to the speaker's audience. Rhetoric also has an influence on the speaker. Catholic leaders are not intentionally trying to manipulate people's emotions, yet the rhetoric they use is also having an impact on them. After having listened to hundreds of people who have been sexually abused, some Catholic leaders are still able to say and genuinely believe that "there is simply never a good reason to leave the Church. Never."[19] In reality, we must respect and trust that people who are choosing to leave are doing so in their best interest. As we have previously argued in the third, fourth, and fifth chapters, in the wake of systemic CPSA it is often necessary for one's health and survival to disaffiliate from the Church. It takes a deeply rooted case of self-idolatry to be unable to see this fact. When someone is confronted with the evidence of their own wrongdoing, or the wrongdoing of their community, that evidence can be experienced as a threat to their worldview and their identity.[20] It should be expected, then, that a Roman

---

[19] Barron, *Letter to a Suffering Church*, 59.

[20] Timothy J. Hodgson and Lindsay B. Carey, "Moral Injury and Definitional Clarity: Betrayal, Spirituality, and the Role of Chaplains," *Journal of Religion and Health* 56, no. 4 (2017): 1212–28.

Catholic leader would employ rhetoric that is meant to pacify himself as much as it is meant to pacify the laity.

As we have pointed out, it would be a mistake to see systemic CPSA as a problem caused and perpetuated by a group of "bad apples."[21] Rather, the rhetorical patterns and images that we have described in this chapter are manifestations of a broader clericalist culture. A culture rooted in clericalism will unsurprisingly cultivate the abuse and oppression of the most vulnerable. The rhetoric of clericalism is the rhetoric of a culture that is essentially oppressive and violent. In order to dismantle such a culture, we must illuminate the rhetorical devices that one can expect to encounter when a violent culture tries to protect itself from being recognized and reformed. Speaking through its most faithful and most loyal adherents, a clericalist culture will employ bracketing in order to distract its critics from the ongoing failures that it cannot defend but cannot live without. It will make excuses and scapegoat the strawmen it wishes were at fault. It will justify itself, insisting that the harm is not as bad as the critics are claiming, especially when compared to how wonderful things could be if people could just choose to forgive and place their hope in the clergy's authority. In short, we can expect to hear rhetoric that refuses to give up its power.

We hope that this chapter can help those who have been affected by systemic CPSA, which is everyone connected to the Catholic Church, to more readily recognize violent rhetoric when it is used by Catholic leadership. We also hope that prioritizing safety and empowerment might aid in the dismantling of the violence that continues to crucify those who have been affected by systemic CPSA.

---

[21] Julie Hanlon Rubio and Paul Schutz, *Beyond 'Bad Apples': Understanding Clergy Perpetrated Sexual Abuse as a Structural Problem and Cultivating Strategies for Change* (Santa Clara, CA: 2022).

Liturgical theology rooted in safety and empowerment is a manifestation of a culture that recognizes the pervasive and damaging nature of trauma. This rhetoric should be a part of our everyday language, transforming clericalist culture and those perceived as leaders. It is meant to be a way of speaking that seeks to transform how systemic CPSA is perceived and how it is treated. This way of speaking is not a response to trauma; it is one piece of a culture that seeks to prevent trauma, promote healing, and cultivate flourishing. Rhetoric that promotes safety and empowerment should replace the status quo and become a pervasive culture itself. It is how someone speaks if they wish to know the true extent, the true causes, and the true remedies for the trauma of systemic CPSA.

8

Seeking Salvation outside the Church

> *Those also can attain to salvation who through no fault of their own do not know the Gospel of Christ or His Church, yet sincerely seek God and moved by grace strive by their deeds to do His will as it is known to them through the dictates of conscience.*
> —DOGMATIC CONSTITUTION ON THE CHURCH, #16

In the previous two chapters we have explored some aspects of clericalist culture that contribute to and exacerbate the traumas of systemic clergy-perpetrated sexual assault (CPSA) while also trying to offer ways toward cultural reforms that might dismantle clericalism and support the healing of those who have been affected by systemic CPSA. In this final chapter we examine the way that clericalist culture uses triumphalism to idolize itself and establish the Catholic Church as the exclusive source of salvation. In the second chapter we pointed out that triumphalism is an "attitude or feeling of victory or superiority" held over others.[1] When someone's hubris leads

---

[1] Merriam-Webster.com Dictionary, s.v. "triumphalism."

them to see everyone else as incapable and inferior adversaries, they are suffering from triumphalism. In the context of religion, triumphalism is the mindset that one's religious tradition is radically unique and superior to all other alternatives. Religious triumphalists would see their own religion as infallible and the only tradition offering complete truth. These believers feel that they are the only truly moral community, the only shining beacon in a world of darkness, the lone ark in a vast flood. Due to this arrogance, a religious triumphalist pejoratively labels people of other religions as heathens, pagans, and infidels. Put differently, triumphalism can lead the Church to insist that it alone is the source of salvation.

This exclusivist stance is no longer official Catholic teaching. The Church has long recognized the possibility of salvation for those who do not belong to the Church. Yet it is all too common to find Catholics (even among the Church's leaders) who believe the contrary.

Since the beginning of Christianity there have consistently been many different ways to describe the relationship between the Church and salvation. One way of understanding this relationship that has arguably existed since the writing of the New Testament is summarized by the Latin phrase *extra ecclesiam nulla salus*, which is often translated into English as "outside the Church, there is no salvation."[2] Basically understood, this doctrine claims that, in order to receive salvation, one must belong to the body of Christ, the Church. For the purposes of this chapter, we refer to these teachings as *exclu-*

---

[2] For an excellent analysis of the origins and development of this doctrine, see Andrew Meszaros, "Extra Ecclesiam Nulla Salus: Lessons for Doctrinal Development Theory in Catholic Theology," *International Journal of Systematic Theology* 24, no. 1 (2022): 100–121; Francis A. Sullivan, *Salvation Outside the Church?: Tracing the History of the Catholic Response* (New York: Paulist Press, 1992).

sivist approaches to salvation. An exclusivist position denies that salvation can come from any source other than Christ and his Church (*LG*, #14).³ This doctrine has many nuanced variations that have developed over the centuries, some more rigidly exclusivist than others.⁴ Yet most exclusivist stances tend to deny the possibility of salvation for those who do not belong to the Church. As such, an exclusivist view of salvation can create a sense of isolation for those suffering from the consequences of systemic CPSA. Our concern here is not with the intricacies of the doctrinal development of this teaching. Rather, our focus is on the fact that many contemporary Catholics, lay and ordained, perpetuate an exclusivist position, believing that those who are not Catholic are going to hell, which is imagined as a very real place where one suffers eternally.

If a Catholic has internalized an exclusivist view of salvation, that doctrine can function as a threat that isolates them from other potential sources of healing and flourishing. Further, an exclusivist view of salvation easily degenerates into a triumphalist attitude that causes members of the Roman Catholic Church to see its ordained ministers and the liturgy they control as the gateways to salvation. As a result, the liturgy becomes an exclusive and obligatory source of grace. As we saw in the previous chapter, this way of describing the liturgy manipulates people's emotions in a manner that weaponizes

---

³ "Whosoever, therefore, knowing that the Catholic Church was made necessary by Christ, would refuse to enter or to remain in it, could not be saved" (*LG*, #14).

⁴ For examinations of the development of Catholic teachings regarding other religions, see Paul F. Knitter, *No Other Name? A Critical Survey of Christian Attitudes toward the World Religions* (Maryknoll, NY: Orbis Books, 1985); Gavin D'Costa, Paul F. Knitter, and Daniel Strange, *Only One Way? Three Christian Responses to the Uniqueness of Christ in a Pluralistic World* (London: SCM Press, 2011).

hope and isolates survivors while cultivating an abusive, clericalist culture. So, in order for the Church to advance the work of deconstructing the clericalist culture of abuse, it must begin to denounce exclusivist teachings that are easily used to manipulate people suffering the impacts of systemic CPSA, better communicate and embody teachings that affirm the possibility of salvation outside the Church, and support and learn from people who choose to leave the Church in search of salvation from the violence they have endured.

Toward this end, this chapter first examines the teachings of the Second Vatican Council on the possibility of salvation outside the Church. Then we argue that the Church must go further, forcefully acknowledging that the traditional culture of the Church has, for some, precluded an experience of God's grace within the Church. Last, we emphasize the need for a process of grief. If those suffering from the consequences of trauma are to courageously seek salvation outside the Church's abusive culture, they must be accompanied and aided in grieving the significant losses that come with walking away from an abusive community and toward healing.

Mitigating Triumphalism: Finding Salvation outside the Church

From 1962 to 1965, as sexual abuse festered in the shadows of cathedrals across the world, an ecumenical council of bishops occurred in Vatican City, resulting in the promulgation of the sixteen documents of the Second Vatican Council. At first glance these two occurrences have little in common. In the United States, for example, priests shielded their abuse behind the veil of clericalism and maintained distance from the lay community. In Rome, debates ensued regarding the relationship between the clergy and laity, how mass ought to be celebrated, and, pivotally, whether and how salvation outside of the Church might be possible. The teachings that emerged from these debates are significant in answering the question of how the Church should respond to the crisis of systemic CPSA. The documents of the Second Vatican Council clearly affirm the possibility of salvation outside the Church, prophetically urging the Church to turn away from the clericalist triumphalism that has inflicted and continues to inflict systemic CPSA.

What follows is a brief survey of texts that explicitly address the possibility of salvation outside the Church. While a literary analysis that centers authors' intents in writing these documents is certainly important, we approach Catholic doctrine as we do scripture: interpretations must shift throughout time to address pressing contemporary situations and contextually appropriate realities. The concerns and contexts of the Catholic Church in 1965 have evolved over the past sixty years. That being said, we interpret these texts through the lens of our concerns regarding the crisis of systemic CPSA. The consequences of trauma that we have discussed throughout this book—post-traumatic stress disorder (PTSD), moral injury, and moral distress—lead us to read these documents as examples of the Church responding to God's demand that the Church better serve the world's need for healing and salvation. Hence, we focus on the question of salvation outside the Catholic Church as a vital question in the shadows of trauma.

When dealing with the traumas inflicted by systemic CPSA, an individual's experience of the liturgy is often drastically changed as a result of the abuse and the culture that facilitated the abuse. However, there remain Catholics (lay and clergy) who hold firm to the common Catholic teaching that one can only achieve salvation through the Catholic Church, even when participation in the liturgy severely harms a person's connection to God. Thankfully, this exclusivist view of salvation is repudiated in multiple places throughout the documents of Vatican II. In its *Decree on Ecumenism* (*Unitatis Redintegratio*) the Council considers the Church's relationship to other Christian churches and communities. This document clearly affirms that Christians who do not belong to the Catholic Church can indeed attain salvation. Further, *Unitatis Redintegratio* affirms the salvific nature of their liturgical celebrations:

> It follows that the separated Churches and Communities as such, though we believe them to be deficient in some respects, have been by no means deprived of significance and importance in the mystery of salvation. These most certainly can truly engender a life of grace in ways that vary according to the condition of each Church or Community. These liturgical actions must be regarded as capable of giving access to the community of salvation. (*UR*, #3)

In other words, the liturgical celebrations of other Christian communities "most certainly . . . must be regarded" as capable of offering the salvific grace of God. Even as the Catholic Church would call these liturgies invalid and/or "deficient in some respects," this should not be understood as a denial of their salvific nature. Remember from the first chapter that Pope Benedict XVI has reaffirmed this teaching of *Unitatis Redintegratio*. Serving in his role as the prefect of the Congregation for the Doctrine of Faith, Joseph Cardinal Ratzinger forcefully made a similar point in a letter written in 1993 to Bavarian Lutheran Bishop Johannes Hanselmann. In his letter the future pontiff emphatically affirmed the efficacy of "invalid" sacraments:

> I count among the most important results of the ecumenical dialogues the insight that the issue of the eucharist cannot be narrowed to the problem of "validity." Even a theology oriented to the concept of [apostolic] succession, such as that which holds in the Catholic and Orthodox church, should in no way deny the saving presence of the Lord in a Lutheran Lord's Supper.[5]

Invalidity of a ritual does not preclude its gracious effects. Hence, a person suffering from the consequences of systemic CPSA who chooses to join a non-Catholic Christian community should never be told that their new community cannot offer salvation. To put it more pointedly, someone like Bishop Robert Barron is plainly incorrect when he says: "Let me state it bluntly: the Eucharist is the single most important reason for staying faithful to the Church. You can't find it anywhere else."[6] As we pointed out in the previous chapter, such rhetoric is not only false, it is abusive language that manipulates the emotions of survivors in order to isolate and control them. A survivor of clericalist culture's cycle of abuse can indeed find the salvific eucharistic presence of Christ outside of the Catholic Church. These teachings from Vatican II can help mitigate the self-idolatrous triumphalism that leads Catholic leaders to insist on an exclusivist vision of salvation where "there is no salvation outside the Church." Instead, a more humble trust in the freedom and mercy of God should be allowed to temper any zeal for one's own perceived superiority.

---

[5] Joseph Ratzinger, "Exchange of Letters between Provincial Bishop Johannes Hanselmann and Joseph Cardinal Ratzinger," in *Pilgrim Fellowship of Faith: The Church as Communion* (San Francisco: Ignatius Press, 2005), 91.

[6] Bishop Robert Barron, *Letter to a Suffering Church: A Bishop Speaks on the Sexual Abuse Crisis* (Park Ridge, IL: Word on Fire, 2019), 74.

While *Unitatis Redintegratio* attests to the possibility of salvation for non-Catholic Christians, there are other places throughout the documents of Vatican II that attest to the possibility of salvation outside of Christianity. Perhaps the most clear declaration in support of salvation outside of Catholicism *and* outside of Christianity comes from the *Dogmatic Constitution on the Church* (*Lumen Gentium*). It states:

> Those who, through no fault of their own, do not know the Gospel of Christ or his Church, but who nevertheless seek God with a sincere heart, and, moved by grace, try in their actions to do his will as they know it through the dictates of their conscience—those too may achieve eternal salvation. (*LG*, #16)

Of utmost importance within this passage is the phrase "through no fault of their own." First, this phrase can be interpreted as referring to people who have not been exposed to the life and teachings of the Church. Such an interpretation understands that the Church is saying that a person who has not experienced the gospel as a provocative offering that calls them to participate in God's friendship is not at fault if they do not belong to the Church. As such, they should not be described as people who are going to Hell, or lacking salvation. Rather, those who have not experienced the gospel can be saved if they seek to do good in the world by following their conscience and continually seeking to know the truth.

Another way of interpreting this phrase, which is more directly related to our concerns, is that ignorance of the gospel can be the result of having one's faith taken from them through abuse and trauma. As we have documented throughout this book, the traumas of systemic CPSA erode a person's faith and agency to the point where the gospel message that is meant to be offered through the celebration of the liturgy (that is, the offering of God's loving friendship) ends up being corrupted. The symbols and language that the Church uses to proclaim the gospel end up meaning something violent instead. The consequences of trauma corrupt the dispositions that are necessary to hear and embrace the offering of God's grace, as it has been proclaimed by the Church. As such, those suffering from trauma can rightfully be described as not knowing the gospel through no fault of their own. More specifically, they do not know the gospel as it is preached by the Church precisely because of the traumas inflicted by the Church's clericalist culture.

Instead of thoughts like "God no longer loves me" or beliefs that they are going to hell because of their inability or unwillingness to participate in the liturgy safely, the phrase "through no fault of their own" can be interpreted as an assurance that their responses to the Church's abuses are not their fault, and that God is still offering them eternal salvation despite their need to walk away from the Church. This passage from *Lumen Gentium* insists that a person's conscience and inherent goodness determine the availability of their salvation, rebuking rhetoric from Catholic leaders who falsely proclaim an exclusivist vision of salvation that demands that trauma survivors stay with the abusive Church. Given these teachings of Vatican II, as people leave the Church, following their conscience to seek healing and happiness, they are, in fact, following God's calls to them and further establishing God's kingdom on earth through their goodness, abilities, and genius.

For those who remain active in the Church, salvation beyond the Catholic Church can still be difficult to understand. While acceptance of an individual's possibility of salvation outside of the Church provides a base level of support, the *Decree of the Mission Activity of the Church* (*Ad Gentes*) describes how the Church ought to handle such departures.

> Although in ways known to himself God can lead those who, through no fault of their own, are ignorant of the Gospel, to that faith without which it is impossible to please him, the Church still has the obligation and also the sacred right to evangelize all men. (*AG*, #7)

What does it mean for a Church that has committed sins like systemic CPSA to evangelize the world? When Catholic leaders become aware of the enormity of their failures, how should that awareness influence the ways that they understand themselves and their mission?

Subverting Triumphalism: No Salvation inside the Church

By acknowledging that salvation is attainable outside the Church, triumphalism begins to diminish. Yet, simply acknowledging this fact is not enough to uproot the self-idolatry that undergirds triumphalism. The Church must go further. It is one thing to acknowledge that there is salvation *outside* the Church; it is another thing to own the fact that, for some, there is no salvation *inside* the Church.

The Second Vatican Council's assertions that salvation is attainable outside of the Catholic Church is indeed critical to our central argument; that is, that those affected by systemic CPSA may struggle to receive God's grace through the liturgy. They ought to be supported in seeking salvation and healing outside of the Catholic Church.

This argument often provokes concern for those leaving the Church. That is, even if it is granted that salvation can be found outside the Church, there is still the belief that, despite the pain inflicted by systemic CPSA, it is better to stay in the Church, precisely because the salvation offered by the Catholic Church is more full and more perfect (*UR*, 3). Again, we can see the similarities to abusive language that manipulates survivors: "He may love you, but he will never love you the way I do." There is a trust in the institution and a sense of superiority that the Catholic Church is better than any alternative. From this triumphalist perspective, staying is always better than leaving, regardless of one's circumstances. For instance, recall Bishop Barron's claim: "There is simply never a good reason to leave the Church. Never."[7] For those who have never experienced PTSD, moral injury, or moral distress as a result of CPSA (and maybe even some who have), it can be tempting to hold the belief that it is better to stay and to fight for the Church than to leave when hurt. Presumably, and most charitably, this comes from a place of love of God and of the Catholic Church and the belief that God's love, grace, and salvation is *best* found within the Catholic Church.[8] However, in light of all that we have discussed thus far, there are people for whom there is *no* salvation inside the Church; they will only find salvation by leaving.

In the third, fourth, and fifth chapters we detailed the subversion of liturgical efficacy due to three consequences of the CPSA crisis: PTSD, moral injury, and moral distress. PTSD rewrites the story of the liturgy for the survivor to be about the trauma they endured instead of communion and relationship with God. Flashbacks and intrusive symptoms caused by PTSD transform the liturgy into something violent. Moral injury drives feelings of betrayal and helplessness in response to the CPSA crisis, shifting one's relationship with God and to the clergy and eroding trust in the Church. Similarly, moral

---

[7] Barron, 74.

[8] Matthew Ramage, "Extra Ecclesiam Nulla Salus and the Substance of Catholic Doctrine: Towards a Realization of Benedict XVI's 'Hermeneutic of Reform,'" *Nova et Vetera* 14, no. 1 (2016): 295–330.

distress alters one's proper predisposition to participate fully and appreciate the liturgy, provoking strong feelings of the worshiper's guilt and powerlessness. These consequences can be felt by laity or clergy, and they may be felt by people with varying proximity to the CPSA crisis. That is, you do not necessarily need to be a survivor of CPSA or know someone who is in order to experience these consequences of CPSA. For those who have felt the impact of the CPSA crisis, the experience of the liturgy is affected, corrupted, and, for some, rendered completely ineffectual. For some, it can even be actively harmful. Given these circumstances, when Catholic leaders encourage belonging to the Catholic Church and participation in the liturgy, they are not evangelizing in a way that saves souls; on the contrary, they are pushing people into situations that further alienate them from God's grace.

The temptation to encourage Church attendance and participation is, as previously stated, often well-meaning and intended for the sake of the healing and salvation. The fear is often, simply put, that the lapsed Catholic is sacrificing their salvation for the temporary comfort of avoiding negative feelings brought on by the liturgy and that this boycott will eventually result in a lack of belief in the Church and in God, thereby undoing their salvation. Hence, as we saw in the previous section, the Second Vatican Council insists that "the Church still has the obligation and also the sacred right to evangelize all men" (*AG*, #7). This obligation is often understood as the need to operate from and proclaim an exclusivist vision of salvation that works by instilling fear and denying the goodness of those outside the Church. We can begin to see why this belief is misguided when we acknowledge that, for many, their experience of the liturgy is destroying their faith and resulting in a form of atheism (or similar feelings of disenfranchisement). In its imperfect form, encouragement to stay in the Catholic Church is motivated by a denial of Vatican II's affirmation of salvation outside of the Church and a presumptuous idolatry that places the liturgical life of the Church (especially the ordained ministers) above God and one's relationship to God. Consciously or not, this push often has more to do with concerns for clerical power and the Church's reputation than true concern and care for a person's salvation. Encouragement (or often, demands) to stay in the Church comes from a fear of losing members and losing control, recognizing, however implicitly, that it is better to have the bodies in the seats regardless of the harm it will cause those people.

In one of his popular online videos, Bishop Robert Barron encouraged Catholics to "stay and fight" rather than leave the Church. In a passionate exhortation, Barron says:

> You fight through your own righteous anger. You fight by writing a letter to your Bishop, a letter to the Pope. You fight by your very presence at Mass. You fight by keeping people's feet to the fire. You fight by organizing your fellow Catholics. Fight any way you can. But you fight because you believe in the Church; you love the Church; and you realize that despite this terrible blight, it's worth fighting for.[9]

It is true that most of the people who have been abused and chosen to leave the Church loved and, for many, continue to love the Church. However, it is a profound mistake to think that their love is a good reason to stay. It is an even more

---

[9] Bishop Robert Barron, "Why Remain Catholic? (With So Much Scandal)," YouTube video, https://www.youtube.com/watch?v=-ani_hnN8Fs, 4:00–4:30.

profound *and abusive* mistake to rhetorically appeal to that love as a means to get them to stay. In reality, a bishop who understands his role as a pastor should not spend his time focusing on the survivor's love of the Church. Instead, they should be focusing on the Church's love for the survivor. If the Church and its leaders truly love those whom they have harmed, then it is their duty to respect the wishes of the survivor and help them find safety, healing, and salvation.

Barron then goes on to use some particularly repugnant language:

> Every one of you listening to me right now who is baptized into Jesus Christ is a prophet. Raise your voice! Prophets didn't cut and run when Israel was in trouble; the prophets spoke out. That's all of our responsibility, all of us who bear the prophetic charism.

To hear a bishop imply that those who are suffering from the consequences of the Church's dehumanizing violence are people who have "cut and run" is disheartening to say the least. Painting survivors as cowards is a particularly cruel way of shaming someone in their time of need. Barron continues:

> But the point is that the Church does not depend ultimately on institutions. We're not fighting primarily for the institutional aspect of the Church's life. We are fighting for the victims of these terrible crimes. We're fighting for people who were sexually assaulted, sexually abused. If we cut and run precisely at this challenging time, who will be the prophetic voice on behalf of these victims?

But Barron fails to address the fact that far more people have been traumatized by the systemic CPSA than those who directly experienced sexual assault. The consequences of systemic CPSA are horrifyingly far-reaching. Second, and more importantly, Barron fails to recognize that *the survivors already have their own prophetic voice.* They are prophesying through their exodus. Barron's assumption that prophetic voices must come from *inside* the Church is an example of the triumphalism and clericalism from which the sexual abuse crisis has grown.

Triumphalist sentiments like this fail to consider that disaffiliation from the Church and a loss of the Catholic faith are less a failure of the one who leaves than it is a failure of the Church and its clericalist culture. In an essay entitled, "The Church and Atheism," Jesuit theologian Karl Rahner explores the motivation of the Church to combat atheism. Rahner explores the notion of the inculpable atheist, achieving salvation outside of the Church, and ultimately posits:

> This struggle against atheism is always and foremost a struggle against a view of God which is in danger of replacing the true, incomprehensible God by a human idol. If there is stupidity and malice even in the Church, this can contribute to such a danger.... The struggle against atheism is foremost and of necessity a struggle against the inadequacy of our own theism.[10]

Here, Rahner does a wonderful job of pointing out that it is often Catholics who, through acts of self-idolatry (e.g., clericalism and systemic CPSA), abusively push people toward atheism and disaffiliation from the Church. There is undoubtedly willful ignorance behind the efforts of Catholic leaders to manipulate people for whom it would cause pain into

---

[10] Karl Rahner, "The Church and Atheism," in *Theological Investigations: Volume XXI* (New York: Crossroad, 1988), 148.

staying in the Church. Clericalism is a pervasive and insidious idolatry, easily and often confused for zeal and piety toward God. And so, when persons, through no fault of their own, are traumatized by this culture of abuse, they can be rendered either explicitly or functionally atheists and no longer able to participate fruitfully in the liturgy with the proper disposition. Their knowledge of God has been corrupted by the acts of the Church clergy who committed heinous acts in God's name.

As we have repeatedly insisted throughout this book, these tragedies are not the fault of the abused and traumatized. The Church's clericalist culture, especially as it is manifested in its liturgical life and its ordained ministers, is responsible for the exodus of people from the Church's abusive control. Their decision to seek healing and peace elsewhere, whether in another Christian community, another religious tradition, or in atheistic/secular contexts, must be seen as an act of courage that reveals the enormity of the Church's sinfulness. Put in liturgical language, the disaffiliation of people harmed by systemic CPSA is itself like a liturgical pilgrimage, an exodus, through which God is calling the harmed to new life *and* calling the Church to conversion.

When a survivor leaves an abuser, the abuser should not beg them to stay (much less demand it). The abuser should have the self-awareness to accept responsibility for the harm done and have the basic decency to support the survivor's search for dignity and health. Of course, this is an exceedingly rare occurrence. Most abusers never experience this self-awareness until they are forced to see themselves honestly. As Pope Francis writes in *Fratelli Tutti*:

> True love for an oppressor means seeking ways to make him cease his oppression; it means stripping him of a power that he does not know how to use, and that diminishes his own humanity and that of others. (*FT*, #241)

Seeking Salvation outside the Church

Clericalists need to be forced to see their abuse and to be stripped of their power. When Catholic leaders refuse to listen and refuse to cease their oppression, sometimes the only way to strip them of their power is to walk away.

In its *Pastoral Constitution on the Church in the Modern World* (*Gaudium et Spes*) the Second Vatican Council humbly acknowledges that those who reject God and religion are often led there by the people who are supposed to preach God's love:

> Undeniably, those who willfully shut out God from their hearts and try to dodge religious questions are not following the dictates of their consciences, and hence are not free of blame; yet believers themselves frequently bear some responsibility for this situation. *For, taken as a whole, atheism is not a spontaneous development but stems from a variety of causes, including a critical reaction against religious beliefs, and in some places against the Christian religion in particular.* Hence believers can have more than a little to do with the birth of atheism. To the extent that they neglect their own training in the faith, or teach erroneous doctrine, or are deficient in their religious, moral or social life, they must be said to conceal rather than reveal the authentic face of God and religion. (GS, #19)

Here, *Gaudium et Spes* draws attention to the responsibility of the Church to non-Catholics. Undoubtedly, clericalism and systemic CPSA have concealed the face of God. The heinous acts of systemic CPSA provide examples of this misrepresentation of God, as is reflected in the lived experience and testimony of survivors whose image of God was deeply damaged by experiences of betrayal, violence, and pain.

When the Church becomes aware of its failures, it must be ready, willing, and grateful to accept the help of people, communities, and institutions that are not counted among the members of the Church. The Church must look outside itself for help. It is no longer simply a matter of encouraging survivors to find the healing and salvation they need elsewhere. The Church must hear God's call to conversion as a call coming from outside itself. The Church must begin to see that, precisely as a pilgrim, its own salvation lies outside itself. The path to its eschatological fulfillment must be illuminated by the divine light that shines outside its own boundaries.

For far too many, there is no salvation inside the Church. When those people find salvation elsewhere—and, thankfully, they do—the Church should seize the opportunity to learn from those sources of salvation. The grace of God thrives elsewhere. Can the Church step away from its own self-idolatry long enough to accept that grace?

Grieving a Loss

In *Abuse and Cover-Up: Refounding the Catholic Church in Trauma*, Gerald Arbuckle examines the many barriers that slow or stop the work of cultural reform. One of the more salient points Arbuckle makes is that the role of grief in cultural change is often overlooked:

> Many changes, even if intellectually agreed to, necessitate loss, and loss evokes the sadness of grief in individuals and cultures. Unless this grief can be publicly articulated in mourning rituals, it will haunt the living and lead to dysfunctional behavior and resistance to cultural change.[11]

When a person becomes aware that leaving the Church is the best option for their health and salvation, that does not mean that their escape will bring unalloyed joy and relief. On the

---

[11] Gerald A. Arbuckle, *Abuse and Cover-Up: Refounding the Catholic Church in Trauma* (Maryknoll, NY: Orbis Books, 2019), 29.

contrary, survivors who manage to get away from their cycles of abuse are often left with grief and a deep sense of loss. If these people are not supported in processing their grief, they can easily find themselves drawn back into the cycle of abuse. Trauma bonds are powerful, and processing grief is one way that those bonds erode. For the Church to support simultaneously those searching for salvation outside of the Church *and* do the work of reforming its own abusive culture, it must learn how to help people grieve.

To understand why grief is so important to this process, we must understand that an abusive relationship, like the unique ones so many Catholics experience in their relationship to the culture and institution of the Catholic Church, is neither all good nor all bad. Specifically, we need to avoid the simplistic stance that a relationship is either all good—and therefore beneficially formative—or all bad—and therefore harmfully deformative. This binary thinking is a common form of analysis that oversimplifies complicated situations in an attempt to help the analyst feel more certain about their understanding. Through such a binary approach, a relationship that has more goodness will have less badness. Relationships and cultures are far more complicated than that. Just as evaluating a person's relationships using a bad/good binary is inadequate, so too is a bipolar spectrum, where the poles "good" and "bad" are seen as competing in a zero-sum game. Instead, we should recognize how relationships have independent measures, similar to a stereo that has one dial for bass and another for treble. A relationship can grow through events that are good and beautiful, and it can also grow through events that are harmful and abusive. When a person recognizes that a relationship is deeply abusive and harmful, they can still be accurately and acutely aware of the wonderful aspects of the relationship. Indeed, these beneficial characteristics of the relationship are precisely what make emotional connections between abusers and survivors possible and powerful.

It is important to conceptualize relationships this way so that we can better make sense of the challenges that come with leaving the Church. When Barron uses St. Paul's metaphor of treasure and vessel to describe the goodness and the evils of Catholicism, respectively, it is akin to saying, "Don't throw the baby out with the bathwater." These metaphors insist that what is good in a relationship can be separated from what is evil in the relationship. And yet, as we have shown throughout this book, we know that this is not the case in the context of abuse and trauma. As we pointed out in the sixth chapter, when we adopt a relational ontology and begin to see our identities as constituted through our relationships, we can recognize that leaving an abusive relationship involves losing an aspect of one's identity that is formed by *both* the harmful *and* beneficial aspects of that relationship. Hence, if a person leaves the Church in order to escape the ongoing consequences of systemic CPSA, it is perfectly normal to feel conflicted. Because of this attachment, it is all the more important for Catholic leaders to be extremely careful not to exploit and manipulate those powerful emotional connections, lest they facilitate the survivor's return to an abusive relationship.

For most Catholics, the Church is much more than a place of worship; it is a source of identity, comfort, and stability. The liturgies, symbols, and clerical structures that can rightly be seen as complicit in systemic CPSA may once have been symbols of belonging. Letting go of this idealized version of the Church, where it is seen as infallible, protective, and pure, can feel like a profound personal loss. This grief gets compounded by the realization that the very structures created to nurture faith are also sources of deep betrayal. Change, even when necessary, often comes with grief and loss. For people who have experienced domestic violence, there is significant, lasting grief that arises from losing one's relationship, sense of self, community, and so much more. Oftentimes, this grief can be so overwhelming that it becomes a compelling reason to stay within the cycle of abuse. For the Catholic Church, transforming the clericalist culture that enables CPSA requires both systemic shifts and an acknowledgment of the emotional and spiritual losses that come with leaving behind traditions, practices, and community that give a person a large part of their identity. Grieving the loss of the Church's culture is an essential part of this healing process, allowing individuals and communities to reckon with the past while struggling to gain a new sense of dignity and agency.

Grief researcher Kenneth J. Doka has used the term *disenfranchised grief* to describe events where a person is denied the right or opportunity to grieve their loss.[12] And Vivienne Elizabeth writes: "In contrast to experiences of culturally validated grief, experiences of disenfranchised grief do not garner sympathy. A common reason for grief experiences to be disenfranchised is a cultural and social failure to recognise that a loss has occurred."[13] People who are experiencing the consequences of systemic CPSA regularly experience disenfranchised grief when their initial abuse is denied and unrecognized. Every time that Catholic leaders seek to protect the power of the ordained ministers by covering up the abuse, making excuses, threatening retaliation, or insisting that survivors should stay in the abusive environment, they deny the survivor their right to grieve. If a person's loss is not publicly acknowledged by truth telling, accountability, and other practices of justice, they are disenfranchised of their grief. At a bare minimum, the Church should be working continually to acknowledge fully and take accountability for

---

[12] Kenneth J. Doka, ed., *Disenfranchised Grief: New Directions, Challenges, and Strategies for Practice* (Champaign, IL: Research Press, 2002).

[13] Vivienne Elizabeth, "'It's an Invisible Wound': The Disenfranchised Grief of Post-Separation Mothers Who Lose Care Time," *Journal of Social Welfare and Family Law* 41, no. 1 (2018): 34–52.

the pain and losses it has inflicted so that people can process their grief in healthy ways.[14]

However, once a survivor's experiences of abuse have been affirmed and they have decided to break ties with the Catholic Church, they are still susceptible to another disenfranchised grief. This time, they may be denied the right to grieve those aspects of the Catholic culture that they loved. A person suffering from the impacts of systemic CPSA can grieve the loss of the liturgy because, to use Bishop Barron's preferred metaphor, it is indeed a treasure.[15] The tragedy is that, while the "treasure" may be *conceptually* different from the "vessel" that carries it, the treasure is *practically* inextricable from the vessel. Such is the nature of embodied rituals like the liturgy; they cannot be properly understood apart from their lived reality. In reality, there is no such thing as a liturgy that is separable from clericalism and systemic CPSA. As we pointed out in the third, fourth, and fifth chapters, the treasure is corrupted because the vessel is abusive. So, precisely because they are inextricable, the treasure deserves grieving even as its vessel deserves repudiation.

As someone who is struggling with consequences of systemic CPSA begins to heal in a new community outside of the Church, it is crucial that the loss of their Catholic identity not be framed as an obvious triumph that requires celebration. For bystanders who have been trying to help a survivor escape an abusive relationship, it can be tempting to insist that the abusive relationship was nothing but harmful. Out of fear that the survivor might return to the cycle of abuse, a friend might emphatically insist that there is nothing good to return to. Yet this language does not take into account the reality of

---

[14] Judith L. Herman, *Truth and Repair: How Trauma Survivors Envision Justice* (London: Basic Books, 2023).

[15] Barron, *Letter to a Suffering Church,* 58–59.

the deep loss that is being experienced. Much like a Catholic leader who desperately tries to manipulate a survivor's love of the Church to keep the person close, a friend who exploits fear in order to keep a survivor safe is also not respecting the agency and experiences of the person they love. When someone leaves the Church, the best way to work against the powerful emotional connections that threaten their health is to help them grieve and assure them that a new, beautiful life is possible. Despite the insistence of many exclusivist Catholics, God's love is not limited to the intentions of Catholic leaders.

When a survivor's abuse isn't acknowledged by the Church, their grief is disenfranchised. We have seen that this is an all-too-common tragedy in the Catholic Church. Yet, when a survivor does choose to leave, if their loss of community or the pain of leaving the tradition they loved is not acknowledged, their disenfranchisement is compounded. Instead of saying, "No. You shouldn't miss the Church. Look at what it did to you," everyone who wants to help survivors, the members of the Church and those outside it, should find ways to affirm that leaving an abusive relationship does involve the loss of something good.

Out of a desire to protect a survivor from returning to an abusive situation that has not changed, it may be tempting to deny their grief and simply define it as symptomatic of a harmful emotional connection. Instead, grief can be facilitated and eased by providing experiences of new possibilities. The weaponized hope that would return the griever's attention to the abusive relationship can be replaced with hope in new possibilities. Celebrating the Lord's Supper at a Lutheran church led by a woman pastor might provide the survivor with a safe and welcoming new environment where they can grieve their loss in the salvific eucharistic presence of Christ. Regularly attending a Jodu Shinshu service at a local Buddhist temple may allow the former Catholic to find a ritual rhythm that offers stability and calm as they seek a renewed sense of peace. Joining a local community theater might provide a community that works to heal and support one another and the larger community through drama and storytelling. A Catholic who wants to support a survivor of systemic CPSA can help preach this message by rooting their own hope in the freedom of God's mercy and unconditional love. The Church should not try to help survivors grieve by affirming its own goodness. Rather, it should affirm the survivor's pain and be a champion of the peace, health, and salvation that is possible outside the Church.

Conclusion: Accepting Grace

Survivors might not be the only ones who need to seek salvation outside the Church. The Church itself must be willing to see the salvific work of God that is taking place outside its own boundaries. Thankfully, God's mercy is being offered to the Church through a salvation history that resists the control of the clergy. The work of the *Boston Globe's* Spotlight journalists should readily be recognized as an activity of the Holy Spirit, reforming the Church and moving her to conversion. As Vatican II has made abundantly clear, God's salvific activities in history are not limited to those undertaken by baptized Christians, much less by ordained ministers. Rather, the Church should be willing to recognize the freedom of God's pervasive and compelling love. If this beautiful truth is joyously preached, then the survivors who are no longer experiencing salvation inside the Church can be accompanied in their grief as they walk away from an abusive home and follow the call of a God who longs for them and who refuses to allow the Church's clericalist culture to define, diminish, and denigrate the good news of salvation and human flourishing.

At its best, the liturgical life of the Church is a breathtakingly beautiful source and summit of friendship with God. The liturgy can be a celebration and offering of God's gratuitous gift of dignity and life. The Church, especially through its liturgical life, certainly can and has been a prophetic voice calling the world more deeply into friendship with God. Yet, for that to continue to be true, the Catholic Church must tirelessly seek to reform itself in the image of the Christ, the one who was willing to hear the challenge of the Syrophoenician woman (Mk 7:24–30) and the one who looks to Samaritans, not religious leaders, for examples of true communion (Lk 10:25–37).

A person who is not open to being transformed by encounters with "outsiders" is an idolater. A person whose God can only be worshiped in a Roman Catholic Church is an idolater. And, idols need sacrifices. As the abusive history of systemic CPSA has shown, Catholic leaders continue to sacrifice vulnerable people to the idol of clerical power. As we have argued throughout this book, the liturgy is often used as a tool to perpetuate these sacrifices. In the shadows of trauma, the liturgy can be used to inflict many kinds of abuse. Yet, from within those shadows, the liturgy might continue to be a source and summit of healing, friendship, and grace. If this is to happen, Catholics must accept the grace that God offers through other sources of light that can destroy the darkness of the Church's clericalist culture.

Index

Abuse and Cover-Up (Arbuckle), 186
Ackerman, Alissa, 63–65, 67, 68, 82
Ad Gentes (*AG*), 177–78, 180
America (periodical), 162
Arbuckle, Gerald, 52, 186
Athanasius of Alexandria, Saint, 6–7
Augustine of Hippo, Saint, 5, 13–15, 105
Aymond, Gregory, 72, 73
baptism, 4, 14, 98, 124, 142
baptismal priesthood, 133–34, 138
Barron, Robert
   on the Eucharist, 156–57, 175
   on not leaving the Church, 158, 179, 181
   trauma of CPSA, not fully acknowledging, 182–83
   treasure in vessels, use of metaphor, 152–53, 154, 188, 190
Belcher, Kemberly, 134
Benedict XVI, Pope
   "The Church and the Scandal of Sexual Abuse," 67–68
   CPSA, not involving the law in investigations of, 36
   liturgical symbols, on survivors' reactions to, 68–69
   pastoral letter to Catholics of Ireland, 98, 155
   Unitatis Redintegratio, affirming teaching of, 174
Beste, Jennifer, 56
bishops, 122, 127, 165
   2023 Synod of Bishops, 141

   authority of bishops as sacramental, 128
   betrayal, creating feelings of, 92
   Church's love for survivors, need for focus on, 182
   in clericalist framework, 39–40, 41–42, 51, 52, 112
   as covering up abuse, 14, 30, 90, 97, 114, 118
   crozier as a symbol of bishop's authority, 35
   episcopate, membership in, 126
   excommunication for assaulting a bishop, 130
   laity participation in synodal process, eschewing, 113
   listening to CPSA survivors, 162
   Orthodox priest's final liturgy, bishop attending, 143–46
   in relational ontology framework, 140, 142
   relationship with diocese, 135–36, 138
   sin, utilizing the language of, 36–37, 47
   in triumphalist framework, 32, 33, 49
   See also Barron, Robert; Second Vatican Council
Bolte, Tom, 161–62
Bonanno, George, 55, 58
Booth, Adam T., 110–11
Boston Globe (periodical), 48, 130, 192
Butler, Sally, 165

Catechism of the Catholic Church (CCC), 12–13, 18
Chauvet, Louis-Marie, 19, 99
Christian, Becky J., 110–11
"The Church and Atheism" (Rahner), 183
Clark, Travis, 72–73
clergy-perpetrated sexual abuse (CPSA), 80, 160, 185
  abusive history of, 193
  accountability, survivors seeking, 45
  betrayal as central to, 78–79, 97, 101, 102
  Catholic identity, as destabilizing, 83–84, 190
  in clericalist culture, 29, 41, 50, 100, 102, 112, 115, 118–19, 131, 138, 153, 158, 164, 169, 172, 189
  court cases, survivors threatening, 43–44
  CPSA flashbacks, 71
  disaffiliation in response to, 46, 67, 155, 166, 178, 184, 188
  disenfranchised grief, experiencing due to, 189
  isolation, CPSA survivors' sense of, 171
  "Letter to the People of God" in response to, 27–28
  listening to survivors of, 76, 139–40, 161–62, 163
  liturgy, affecting the experience of, 54, 59, 74, 96, 98, 141, 152, 165, 180
  moral distress in the context of, 105, 110
  moral injury resulting from, 82, 85, 87, 90, 91–92, 93, 95, 179
  PTSD as a symptom of, 66, 73, 74
  relocation of abusive clerics, 40–41, 130
  rhetoric aimed at CPSA survivors, 147–48, 149, 150, 156, 167–68
  salvation for CPSA survivors, 175
  self-image of survivors, causing devastation to, 81, 89
  support for survivors of systemic CPSA, 192
  theology of ordained ministry as addressing, 137–43
  trauma, as inflicting, 24, 58, 69–70, 74, 176, 182–83
  treat-the-symptoms response to, 75
  triumphalism and, 35–37, 173
  weaponizing hope against CPSA survivors, 158
clericalism, 106, 133, 192
  as an abusive culture, 24, 131, 148, 175, 185
  bracketing, employing to distract, 152–53, 167
  clericalist self-idolatry, 163
  describing and defining, 30
  grace and clericalism, 22, 71, 164
  hierarchical imbalance of, 162
  impunity of clerics, 42–49
  interchangeability of ordained ministers, 37–42, 43
  light as destroying the darkness of, 193
  liturgy, clericalist approach to, 17, 74, 116, 122–23, 151, 168, 190
  moral character of clericalists, 87
  moral distress and clericalist culture, 84, 110–15, 159
  moral injury resulting from, 94, 159
  power and control of clerics, 16, 124, 149
  real presence of death in clericalist culture, 73
  reform of clericalist culture, 121, 160
  relational ontology and, 139, 141, 143
  sexual abuse crisis, as fostering, 28, 129
  in substance ontology framework, 130, 131–32, 136, 142, 154
  systemic CPSA, role in, 29, 41, 50, 100, 102, 112, 115, 118–19,

Index

131, 138, 153, 158, 164, 169, 172, 189
trauma, clericalism as facilitating, 50–52, 53, 71, 169, 177, 184
triumphalism of clericalist culture, 31–37, 43, 173, 183
violence inflicted by clericalist culture, 59
Clohessy, David, 16–17
Code of Canon Law, 130
Collins, Marie, xvii–xviii
compassion fatigue, 111
complicity, doctrine of, 114–15
concept creep, 55–56
confirmation, sacrament of, 4, 124
Constitution on the Sacred Liturgy. See *Sacrosanctum Concilium*
Cozzens, Donald, 162–63
crescendo effect, 113
culture of death, 101, 105, 146
clericalism, describing as, 29, 30, 49, 123
"Letter to the People of God," mentioned in, 28
liturgical efficacy, as subverting, 71, 75, 117
moral injury, making possible in, 97
Pope Francis as noting, 50, 53–54, 93, 123
purpose of liturgy amid, 52
sexual-abuse crisis as a consequence of, 51, 112, 114
Dallas Charter (USCCB), 50–51
deacons, 104, 126
Decree of the Mission Activity of the Church. See *Ad Gentes*
Decree on Ecumenism. See *Unitatis Redintegration*
desecration, 71–72
DeVille, Adam, 135
Devos Barlem, Edison Luiz, 107–8
Diagnostic and Statistical Manual of Mental Disorders (DSM), 60–61, 65, 81
Diocletian, Emperor, 14
disenfranchised grief, 189–90
dissociation, 61, 62–64, 65

Dogmatic Constitution on the Church. See *Lumen Gentium*
Doka, Kenneth J., 189
Donatism, 14, 15, 100
Doyle, Thomas, 40, 44–45, 46, 91–92
Easton, Scott, 79, 89
Eco, Umberto, 42–43
Elizabeth, Vivienne, 189
Epstein, Elizabeth Gingell, 113
Erickson, Ashley, 88
Eucharist, 74, 103, 117
Barron on, 152, 156–57, 175
divine life of Christ, as participation in, 102
Eucharistic sacrifice, 16, 34
grace, as meant to communicate, 73
paten and chalice used to celebrate, 127, 137
PTSD, experiencing during celebration of, 68, 69
Roman Rite as Latin version of the Eucharist, 104
salvific eucharistic presence of Christ, 191
seven sacraments, as part of, 4
in substance ontology lens, 124
traditional eucharistic theology, 145
validity of the eucharistic sacrament, 21
Evangelium Vitae (EV), 28
ex opere operato (from work having been worked), 13–14
extra ecclesiam nulla salus (outside the Church, no salvation), 170
faith, 98, 178, 188
of CPSA survivors, 80, 89, 176–77, 180
early Christians' renunciation of faith, 14
Eucharist as source and summit of Catholic faith, 103
liturgy as inspiring faith, 23, 78
losing faith, 101–2, 183
moral injury as shaking faith, 77, 80, 95, 99, 105, 114, 118
in triumphalist framework, 32

Finch, Jon, 55
Fink, 15–16, 20
flashbacks
  abreaction as flashback moments, 62–63
  avoidance of liturgy to avoid flashbacks, 69–70, 96
  clergy as triggering flashbacks, 67, 69, 141
  crucified Body of Christ and, 76
  intent of the liturgy, as subverting, 65–66, 71
  PTSD, as a symptom of, 61, 64–65, 67, 82, 96, 179
Francis, Pope
  on clericalism, 32, 124, 132
  culture of death, noting, 50, 53–54, 93, 123
  Fratelli Tutti on oppressors, 184
  laity, granting voting rights to, 141
  "Letter to the People of God," 27–28, 50
  Synod on Young People, opening address, 137
  synodal approach, on the need for, 113
  triumphalism, warning against, 35
Fratelli Tutti (FT), 184
Frawley-O'Dea, Mary, 45–46
funerals, 4, 98, 131
Gaillardetz, Richard, 38, 125–26, 133, 134, 135
Gaudium et Spes (GS), 185
Gauthe, Gilbert, 44
grace, 176, 177, 186
  accepting grace, 38, 192–93
  alienation from God's grace, 180
  Christ's grace as a treasure, 152
  the Church, grace experienced within, 135, 172, 179
  clerics as conduits for grace, 140
  cultivating grace, 22–25, 53, 73
  dispensing grace, 12–17, 34, 38, 39, 74, 164
  laity as instruments of grace, 138
  liturgy as a source of grace, 10, 53, 77, 78, 93, 100, 116, 132, 151, 154, 159, 171, 174, 178
  offering of grace in the liturgy, 17–22, 118
  in substance ontology framework, 122, 128
  summit of grace, 11–12, 17, 19, 22, 24–25, 52, 54, 59, 71, 77, 131, 164
Guido, Joseph J., 80
Hadley, Christopher, 134
Halicek, Megan, 88
Hamric, Ann Baile, 113
Hanselmann, Johannes, 21, 174
Herman, Judith L., 40–41, 63, 130–31
identity, 138, 166, 189
  bishops, identity of, 136
  Catholic identity, 98–99, 102, 188, 190
  CPSA survivors, destabilized identity of, 83–84
  indelible characters as markers of identity, 125
  ministers' identity with Christ, 16, 34
  moral injury as damaging to, 80–81, 83, 84, 87–88, 91, 93, 95
  priests, identity of, 127, 128
  self-identity, 79, 82, 89
  shared community identity, 11, 148
  in substance ontology context, 123, 126
  in triumphalist framework, 32, 37
in persona Christi capitis (in the person of Christ, the head), 33–34, 35
indelible spiritual character, 124–25, 126, 128, 132, 137, 139, 141
Ite, missa est (Go, the mass has ended), 104
Jameton, Andrew, 107
Jesus Christ, 130, 146, 193
  body of Christ, 36, 41, 68–69, 76, 102, 132, 170
  clerics as symbols of Christ, 34, 66, 73, 89, 96, 145

Index

communion of the Church, encountering Christ in, 155
dignity of Jesus Christ, emulating, 161
eucharistic presence of Christ, 157, 175, 191
faith as necessary for disciples of Christ, 105
followers of Christ as prophets, 182
Gospel of Christ, 176
grace, Christ as the source of, 15
as the Head of the Church, 128, 133
liturgy, encounter with Jesus via, 5–7, 10, 11, 17, 24, 78, 103–4, 152
living as Christ's presence in the world, 78, 116, 137
love of Christ, 10, 12, 39, 51
presence of Christ in liturgy, 14, 16, 144–45
priesthood of Christ, 134
in relational ontology framework, 139
salvation through Christ, 171
John Paul II, Pope, Saint, 28, 29, 36, 128
Jones, Serene, 57
Karst, Layla, 72
Keenan, James, 42
Kerig, Patricia, 81, 84
laicization, 73
laity, 46, 113, 135, 137, 166
clergy as set apart from, 34, 35, 130, 131
in clericalist context, 16, 22, 30, 41, 49, 75, 93, 112, 129, 146, 151, 153
Cozzens on the voice of the laity, 162–63
Dallas Charter, role of laity in, 50
grace as dispensed to the laity, 13, 38, 39
lay collaboration, importance of, 136
liturgical obligations, laity filling, 116–17
liturgy, lay participation in, 2–3, 8, 9, 17, 51
moral distress of the laity, 109, 115, 180
moral injury, laity experiencing, 84
ordained ministry in service of the laity, 132–33
priests, laity's view of, 96–97
in relational ontology framework, 122, 134, 138–42
relationship of laity with priests, 127–28, 144, 172
rhetoric as pacifying the laity, 167
sexual-abuse crisis, lay reflection on, 29–30, 106
in triumphalist framework, 36
weaponizing hope against the laity, 158
latae sententiae (excommunication), 130
Law, Bernard, 130–31
leaving the Church
Barron on not leaving the faith, 158, 179, 181
Benedict letter exhorting survivors not to leave, 155
Catholic leaders discouraging leaving, 148, 166, 177
challenges that come with leaving, 188
grief and loss upon leaving, 186–87, 191
for salvation from CPSA violence, 172
in triumphalist framework, 178
unconditional love of God for those who leave, 165
Leone-Sheehan, Danielle, 79
Letter to a Suffering Church (Barron), 152
liturgy, 112, 127, 130
Christ's presence in the liturgy, 144–45
clericalist culture as impeding the liturgy, 51, 121–23
as a communal activity, 160–61

describing and defining, 3–12
in early Christianity, 38–39
Eucharist, importance to liturgical life, 103–4
flashbacks as subverting experience of, 65–66
grace, cultivating through liturgy, 22–25
grace, dispensing through liturgy, 12–17, 34, 74
grace, liturgy as a source of, 10, 53, 77, 78, 93, 132, 171, 178
grace, liturgy as the summit of, 11, 12, 17, 18, 19, 22, 24–25, 52, 54, 59, 71, 77, 131, 164, 193
grace, offering through liturgy, 17–22
liturgical efficacy, moral injury as hindering, 80, 94, 95–101
liturgical efficacy, PTSD subverting, 59, 60, 61, 62, 66–73, 75, 179
liturgical life of the Church, placing above God, 181
liturgical participation as obligatory, 147, 148, 165–66, 173
liturgical renewal, 1–3
loss of the liturgy for grieving CPSA survivors, 188, 190
moral distress and, 105–6, 115–18, 179–80
ordination liturgy, 37, 126, 134–35
in relational ontology framework, 139, 141, 142–43, 146
rhetorical manipulation and liturgy, 151–59
Sacrosanctum Concilium on, 10
salvific nature of the liturgy, 20, 122, 151, 164, 174
in substance ontology framework, 128, 129
trauma as damaging liturgical life, 53–54, 102, 177, 184
Litz, Brett, 81, 84
Lumen Gentium (LG), 16, 34, 136, 171, 176, 177
Mancini, Anthony, 55, 58

Markham, Chelsea, 88–89
Mediator Dei (MD), 23
Mescher, Marcus, 82
injury, describing and defining, 78
on moral injury as a concept in development, 85
taxonomy of moral injury, 86–94
moral distress
agency, deleterious effect on, 142
clericalist culture and, 110–15, 122, 159
cultural change, viewing as impossible, 119
describing and defining, 106–10
liturgical efficacy, as hindering, 115–18, 179–80
manipulative rhetoric as exacerbating, 147, 148
sexual-abuse crisis, as a consequence of, 105, 179
trauma, as an effect of, 59, 173
moral injury, 114, 159, 179
betrayal-based moral injury, 86, 87–89, 141
as a concept in development, 106
describing and defining, 78–85
different types of, 85–95
failure to act, 89–90, 94
harmful effects of, 111
institutional affiliation, 91–92, 94
liturgical efficacy, as hindering, 77, 95–101, 102, 118, 122
manipulative rhetoric as exacerbating, 147, 148
moral distress, distinguishing from, 110
perpetration-based moral injury, 86–87
sacred moral injury, 94–95
toxic environment, arising from exposure to, 92–94
trauma, moral injury as an effect of, 59, 142, 173
moral residue, 110–11, 115
moral resignation, 116, 118
Name of the Rose (Eco), 42–43
Nassar, Larry, 88

Noceti, Serena, 136
Nolan, David, 139–40
O'Leary, Patrick, 79
ontological change, 125
ordination, rites of, 126–29
Parzyck, Valerie, xv–xvii
Pastoral Constitution on the Church in the Modern World. See *Gaudium et Spes*
Paul, Saint, 9, 188
Paul VI, Pope, Saint, 1
Pius XII, Pope, 22–23, 127
post-traumatic stress disorder (PTSD), 148, 159, 173
  agency, deleterious effects on, 142
  describing and defining, 59–66
  as a diagnostic concept, 56, 81
  flashbacks associated with, 61, 64–65, 96, 179
  liturgical efficacy, subverting, 54, 66–73, 75, 77, 78, 100, 122
  liturgy attendance for PTSD sufferers, 74, 105, 147
  moral distress arising with, 109–10, 111
  moral injury and, 84, 87
  presence of ordained ministers as triggering, 141
  PTSD flashbacks, 61, 64–65, 67, 82, 96, 179
praebetur (dispensed), 12, 13
presbyters, 41–42, 67, 126, 127
Priest, Pastor, and Minister of the Parish Community (PPM), 128
Rahner, Karl, 183
Ratzinger, Joseph, 20–21, 174
Reid, Joan, 149
relational ontology
  clericalism and, 141–42
  dignity of the clergy, highlighting, 139, 140
  loss of identity, recognizing, 188
  ordained ministry rooted in, 132–37, 143, 145–46
  substance ontology, differing from, 122
  systemic CPSA, addressing, 137–38

rhetorical violence
  abusive rhetorical appeals, 182
  avoiding rhetorical violence, 147, 159, 166, 168
  in clericalist culture, 167
  cycles of abuse and rhetorical manipulation, 148–50
  isolation resulting from, 157
  liturgy and rhetorical manipulation, 151–59
Rodriguez, Deborah, 66–67
Ronan, Dan, 45
Rubio, Julie Hanlon, 30, 38
sacraments, 97, 128, 139
  clergy, sacramental authority of, 89
  efficacy of, 12, 13–14, 21, 174–75
  holy orders, 4, 124, 125, 126, 127, 137, 152
  sacramental theology, 15, 63, 103, 124, 129, 131
  seven sacraments, liturgical celebration of, 4
Sacramentum Ordinis (SO), 127
sacrilege, 72
Sacrosanctum Concilium (SC), 1–3, 6, 8, 10, 11, 20, 23
salvation, 102, 146, 152
  afterlife salvation, temptation to focus on, 119
  as becoming more like God, 7
  in clericalist culture, 16, 33, 97, 131, 148, 157, 159
  exclusivist approaches to, 155–56, 169, 170–72, 175
  invalid liturgy as offering salvation, 71
  laity, role in salvation of all, 38, 142
  liturgy, salvific value of, 20, 122, 151, 164, 174
  mortal sin as jeopardizing salvation, 160
  salvation outside the church, 112, 172–73, 174, 176, 177, 178–86, 187, 192
Scarsella, Hilary Jerome, xix–xx
Schutz, Paul, 30, 38

Second Vatican Council, 133, 180, 192
  Gaudium et Spes, 185
  liturgical celebration, focus on, 116
  on priests in the early church, 125
  Sacrosanctum Concilium, 1–3
  on salvation outside the church, 172–73, 174, 176, 177, 178, 181
  triumphalism, mitigation of, 175
secularism, 28
Shanley, Paul, 40–41
Shay, Jonathan, 81
sin, 43, 124, 184
  liturgy as addressing, 123
  nonattendance at mass as a mortal sin, 160
  paternalistic pity for sinners, 31
  rhetoric and messages of sinfulness, 148
  sexual crimes as sinful, 36–37, 47
  structures of sin in Catholic culture, 29
  systemic CPSA as a sin, 178
  unfortunate sins, equating abusive behaviors with, 157
Souza Ramos, Flávia, 107–8
Sperry, Len, 94, 95
Spotlight (film), 48, 130
Starkey, A. Denise, 99, 148
substance ontology
  of clericalism, 141–42, 154
  ordained ministry in framework of, 123–32, 157
  relational ontology and, 122, 136, 137
  in relationship to the Church, 133
suicidal ideation, 80, 83
theosis (divinization), 7
Thomas Aquinas, Saint, 10, 124–25, 137
traditio instrumentorum, 127–28
trauma, 166, 172, 188
  clericalism as facilitating, 29, 41, 50–52, 71, 101, 122, 184
  consequences of traumatic events, 77, 173, 179
  CPSA as causing, 35–36, 150, 168, 169, 176–77, 182–83
  describing and defining, 54–59, 60–62
  healing trauma through relational ordained ministry, 137–43
  in the life of the Church, 24, 74–75, 76
  liturgy, trauma as damaging, 53, 105, 121, 193
  moral distress, trauma as leading to, 109
  moral injury and, 81, 85, 87, 96, 100, 102
  suicide deaths resulting from trauma, 131
  trauma bonds, 149, 187
  trauma-informed care, 159, 161, 163
  traumatic flashbacks, 63, 64, 69–70
triumphalism
  clericalist culture, as a marker of, 37, 42, 43
  describing and defining, 31, 169–70
  entitlement, promoting a sense of, 47, 49, 51
  fears of negative publicity, combining with, 46
  on ministers and liturgy as gateways to salvation, 171
  mitigating triumphalism, 172–78
  religious triumphalists, 31–32, 170
  subverting triumphalism, 178–86
  theological language engaging in, 33–36
Truth and Repair (Herman), 40–41, 63, 130–31
"*A Unique Betrayal*" (Guido), 80
Unitatis Redintegratio (*UR*), 174, 176, 179
Van der Kolk, Bessel, 62, 64, 70, 71
Vatican II. *See* Second Vatican Council
weaponized hope, 151–56, 158